NINE
WORDS

A Bible Study to Help You Become
the-Best-Version-of-Yourself®

ALLEN R. HUNT

DynamicCatholic.com
Be Bold. Be Catholic.®

NINE WORDS

First Edition
Copyright © 2012 Allen R. Hunt
Published by BEACON PUBLISHING

ISBN: 978-1-937509-35-4

The Best Version of Yourself®
is a registered trademark of The Matthew Kelly Foundation.
Dynamic Catholic® and Be Bold. Be Catholic.®
are registered trademarks of The Dynamic Catholic Institute.

Design by Shawna Powell

For more information on this title and other books
and CDs available through the Dynamic Catholic Book Program,
please visit: www.DynamicCatholic.com

Printed in the United States of America.

TABLE OF CONTENTS

To Thing 1 and Thing 2.
They are God's greatest blessing to me.

All Scripture references are from the
New American Bible unless otherwise noted.

Prologue

YOUR DESTINY IN NINE WORDS

If you had met Johnny in 1995, you would not have been impressed to say the least. Living on the street, addicted to multiple substances, jobless, and estranged from his children, Johnny's life was a mess. He may have had big dreams at some point in his life, but if he had, certainly none of them had come to fruition. Given the range of possibilities for his life, Johnny sadly had settled into the worst possible version of himself: homeless addict who has abandoned his own children.

By 2005, Johnny looked completely different. Clean-shaven, married for the second time, caring for his children from his previous relationships as well as those from his new wife's earlier marriages, Johnny held a full-time job as a meter reader and owned his own modest home. More significantly, Johnny was sober. In fact, he was a leader in his faith community, a diligent pray-er, a generous giver, and an eager volunteer anytime his parish needed his talents and passions.

What had happened? How did Johnny go from a pile of ruined dreams to a man rapidly becoming the-best-version-of-himself? Two moments fundamentally changed Johnny's life. Those two moments provided the springboards for a complete re-making of Johnny's life from the inside out, from broken rubble to budding saint. First, a stranger met Johnny on the street and convinced him that his life had great potential. That God intended more for Johnny's life than for him to be an addict, absentee father, and aimless wanderer. That stranger invited Johnny into his home and offered Johnny a chance to begin again.

Second, through that stranger's compassionate hospitality, Johnny came to a new place in his Catholic faith. Johnny discovered that God did have high hopes and big dreams for his life, that God had indeed created Johnny to be the-best-version-of-himself. By earnestly studying the Scriptures with his fellow believers, and embracing the nine words of Saint Paul that form the foundation of this book, Johnny put into place new patterns and habits in his life that created total transformation in his life.

The unconditional love and aid of a stranger combined with nine powerful words to spur Johnny onto a new journey, one that literally changed his life in almost every way imaginable. A new destiny birthed out of nine words.

I have been privileged to observe firsthand some of Johnny's transformation as well as the change that has occurred in the life of a young man named Art. The path for Art has been quite different than the one Johnny has experienced. Art has many gifts from God, and he has long known it, even in spite of his not being fully sure how to use those gifts. Handsome and hard-working, Art has carved out a fine life for himself. He owns his own business, is recently married, and leads a comfortable life materially. When Art reached his thirty-second birthday, however, he began to ask the more challenging questions of his life. Is this all there is? What does God really desire from my life? Do I have any higher purposes other than running a business and being a faithful husband?

Not long after that birthday, Art began to focus his mind and energy on the nine words that provide the centerpiece of this Bible study. Seeking to become the-best-version-of-himself, Art discovered that these nine words of Scripture gave him a roadmap for doing just that. In seeking to grow in these nine words, Art would now tell you that he is on the way to his destiny.

Certainly not there yet but making good progress. He has discovered a deeper sense of calling and a higher aim for his life, where
he works daily to grow into the-best-version-of-himself.

Nobody grows up wanting to lead a meaningless or unsatisfy-
ing life. No one yearns to be incomplete or frustrated or to lack
any sense of a destiny or purpose. Who would want that? Deep
within each of us, God has implanted the desire to be the-best-
version-of-ourselves. God has a dream for your life. And His
dream for you is unique. Only you are you. And only you can become the-best-version-of-yourself.

If you could describe the-best-version-of-yourself in just nine
words, what would those nine words be? Which ones would you
pick? Perhaps some from this list: Successful. Happy. Purposeful.
Friendly. Parent. Helpful. Fulfilled. Holy.

Saint Paul uses nine words to achieve just that: to describe
the-best-version-of-yourself. In fact, in his letter to the Galatians,
the apostle paints a very clear picture of the destiny God has in
mind for you. He captures that destiny by contrasting two ways
of life: the way of the flesh and the way of the Spirit.

What defines the way of the flesh? Paul makes a list, descrip-
tions that you might even call the-worst-version-of-yourself.
"Immorality, impurity, licentiousness, idolatry, sorcery, hatreds,
rivalry, jealousy, outbursts of fury, acts of selfishness, dissensions,
factions, occasions of envy, drinking bouts, orgies, and the like."

Then he goes for the heart. He draws the target for you, what
the-best-version-of-yourself will look like. This is your destiny.
He calls these words the fruit of the Spirit (Gal. 5:22–23) because
these nine words encompass the way of the Spirit, the way God
intends for your life.

Love. Joy. Peace.

Patience. Kindness. Generosity.

Faithfulness. Gentleness. Self-control.

That's it. Nine words. A portrait of your destiny, the dream God has for your life. Some call it holiness. Others call it being conformed to the image of Christ. Saint Paul calls it the fruit of the Spirit. You might just call it the-best-version-of-yourself.

Whatever you call your destiny, these nine words provide the blueprint. And I have designed this simple study to help you dive into God's dream and grow into the-best-version-of-yourself.

Introduction

WHY CHRISTIANS ARE DIFFERENT

Christians are different. Or at least they should be.

After all, as the apostle Paul says, *"I have been crucified with Christ; yet I live, no longer I, but Christ lives in me."* (Gal. 2:20) What a revolutionary idea: As a Christian, you have been crucified with Christ. He now lives in you. That means you no longer live by the world's standards; instead, you live by faith in the Son of God. Your values will differ from the values of the world. When the world says, "If it feels good, do it," Jesus says, *"Deny yourself and follow me."* When the world says, "I gotta be me," Jesus says, *"You are my sheep, my flock."* When the world says, "Do unto others, and then split," Jesus says, *"Do unto others as you would have them do unto you."* To follow Jesus is to be different.

In other words, Jesus wants your heart and your soul. He yearns to free you from the awful bondage of serving only yourself and seeking only your own advantage. He envisions yours as a heart that desires God and His pleasure most of all.

That's what Saint Paul means in Galatians 5:16 when he says, *"Live by the Spirit, I say, and do not gratify the desires of the flesh."* The-best-version-of-yourself will live by faith in God rather than faith in yourself or in the powers of this world. As a result, your behaviors, values, and priorities will change.

God's destiny for you is a life in the Spirit. Saint Paul describes that destiny as fruit, the fruit of God's Spirit. Jesus offers that kind of life to you. How does that happen? True life really begins when the fruit of God's Holy Spirit begin to grow in your heart and life. As those fruit grow, Jesus will change you and me from the inside out.

These nine fruit of God's Spirit are the focus of this study. Notice that the apostle Paul says "fruit" of the Spirit rather than "fruits." He uses the singular, not the plural. He does this because God does not give you just one or a few of the fruit. Rather, God begins to bring all of these fruit to reality in your life as you seek Him. That is the work of the Holy Spirit in you. We do not pick and choose the fruit; God intends to give them all to each of us. After all, they are your destiny. These nine words capture the-best-version-of-yourself.

These fruit may grow at different rates and at different times in our spiritual lives, but each of us can and will experience growth in all of them to some degree. In other words, when you live in the Spirit of God, you will begin to watch love, joy, peace, patience, kindness, generosity, faithfulness, gentleness, and self-control blossom in your life. That is how you will know that you are growing into the-best-version-of-yourself: You will notice more of God's fruit in your life.

In this study, I guide you through each fruit of the Spirit. Each chapter seeks to paint what that spiritual fruit looks like in real life.

My goal is not only to grow your understanding of each fruit but also to provide practical, real life tips that you can use to allow these fruit to blossom in your daily life. After all, that is your goal: to become the-best-version-of-yourself. At the end of each chapter, therefore, I have provided five ways to increase that fruit in your own life. All in all, a total of forty-five tips populate the entire study to move you toward the-best-version-of-yourself.

God desires no more and no less than for your heart to belong to Him. God dreams that you will become the-best-version-of-yourself. He wants these fruit of His Spirit to abound in your life.

God gives you His Spirit; Jesus has promised you that He lives within you. Turn that power loose in how you live. And then become the-best-version-of-yourself!

As you begin this study to move toward the-best-version-of-yourself, start with a short self-evaluation. How would you rank yourself in each of the fruit? Circle the number of how much you see this fruit prospering in your life, with a score of 1 being very little and 10 being the fullest abundance you could ever imagine. Doing this will help you envision where and how you will grow as you seek to become the-best-version-of-yourself.

Love	1 • 2 • 3 • 4 • 5 • 6 • 7 • 8 • 9 • 10
Joy	1 • 2 • 3 • 4 • 5 • 6 • 7 • 8 • 9 • 10
Peace	1 • 2 • 3 • 4 • 5 • 6 • 7 • 8 • 9 • 10
Patience	1 • 2 • 3 • 4 • 5 • 6 • 7 • 8 • 9 • 10
Kindness	1 • 2 • 3 • 4 • 5 • 6 • 7 • 8 • 9 • 10
Generosity	1 • 2 • 3 • 4 • 5 • 6 • 7 • 8 • 9 • 10
Faithfulness	1 • 2 • 3 • 4 • 5 • 6 • 7 • 8 • 9 • 10
Gentleness	1 • 2 • 3 • 4 • 5 • 6 • 7 • 8 • 9 • 10
Self-control	1 • 2 • 3 • 4 • 5 • 6 • 7 • 8 • 9 • 10

Now add together the numbers you have circled. A score of 9 would indicate you have a long way to grow to become the-best-version-of-yourself. A score of 90 would suggest that you have totally self-actualized! Your score will likely be somewhere between 40 and 60.

Set a goal to use the real-life suggestions at the end of each chapter/lesson to improve your self-evaluation by a total of nine points in the coming nine weeks of study on these lessons. You may grow each fruit by one point or pick a few in which you see a large need to leap forward by three points each. Do what is most helpful to you, but set a goal to ensure that you have a target in mind to inspire you forward.

You will discover that the best way to use this Bible study is to keep this original self-scoring in mind as you read and reflect on Scripture. Your goal is to grow nine points. And as you have fun doing so, you will find greater satisfaction in living because you will be moving toward the target: the-best-version-of-yourself.

LOVE

"... the fruit of the Spirit is LOVE, joy, peace, patience, kindness, generosity, faithfulness, gentleness, self-control ..." Galatians 5:22–23

1. THE MOST EXCELLENT WAY
Love God. Love People.

Love makes a difference. It's the difference between life and death.

Love's difference can be best seen in babies born either addicted to drugs such as cocaine or suffering from deadly diseases such as AIDS. The odds are stacked drastically against them. With a mother addicted or infected, a newborn infant receives little or no interaction, affection, or stimulation. As a result, these infants fail to thrive. The first few weeks of life often present more challenges to the life of the baby than his or her small body can withstand. With the body ravaged by chemical dependency or deadly disease, the newborn struggles to stay alive.

To combat these seemingly insurmountable odds against life, many hospitals and medical teams use a creative strategy: They recruit volunteers to stop by daily simply to hold, touch, and speak to these uniquely challenged newborn human beings. The results surprise even the most advanced medical researchers. By providing attention and loving care for the infants, these volunteers increase the addicted infants' rate of survival dramatically. As the volunteers reach out to newborns who receive little or no other affectionate attention, fewer infant deaths occur. Fewer children succumb to "failure to thrive," the medical term for the inability to gain momentum in living.

The truth is plain: Love makes the difference.

Put simply, humans need love. Without it, you will die. Failure to thrive really means "failure to be loved."

Frederick II discovered this truth in a unique way when he ruled in the thirteenth century. He wanted to test babies to discover what language they would speak if they never interacted with adults but only with each other. Would they communicate in Latin or in Greek or in some other language unknown to adults? To find out, Frederick ordered a group of infants quarantined—separated from all adults other than a lone nurse who silently changed their diapers and provided some food each day. She interacted with the newborns for only the most basic needs: food and cleanliness. She offered no kind touches, no words of affection, no smiles. Essentially, having no interaction with a loving caregiver meant the children received no love.

As a result, Frederick was shocked when the babies did not learn to communicate with each other. Instead, they died. No love meant death. Instead of learning what language they would develop, Frederick discovered that without the love of a mother or caring adult, the children could not survive. Failure to thrive, absence of love, death—the truth emerged plainly: Love is essential for our lives.

That's where the Christian faith comes in. In the first century, Christians were certainly not the only organized group in the Roman world. Dinner groups met for social purposes. Burial societies were organized to provide social interaction and preparation of post-death arrangements. Philosophical schools created opportunities for people to gather around gifted teachers to pursue education and intellectual achievement. Pagan cults sought to give meaning to life through their seasonal rituals and sacrifices to the gods.

However, Christians were the only group governed and

centered by the principle of love, the Greek word *agape*. The early Christians built their foundation on the idea of agape love. Agape love is selfless love. Generous love. Sacrificing love.

Perhaps that's why the most famous words ever written about love emerged from the mouth of a Christian. Saint Paul describes love as the highest and best spiritual gift to be experienced in this lifetime:

But I shall show you a still more excellent way.

*If I speak in human and angelic tongues, but do have not **love**, I am a resounding gong or a clashing cymbal. And if I have the gift of prophecy, and comprehend all mysteries and all knowledge, if I have all faith, so as to move mountains, but do not have **love**, I am nothing. If I give away everything I own, and if I hand my body over so that I may boast but do not have **love**, I gain nothing.*

***Love** is patient, **love** is kind. It is not jealous, **love** is not pompous, it is not inflated, it is not rude, it does not seek its own interests, it is not quick-tempered, it does not brood over injury, it does not rejoice over wrongdoing but rejoices with the truth. It bears all things, believes all things, hopes all things, endures all things.*

***Love** never fails.* (1 Corinthians 12:31–13:8a)

Saint Paul's thoughts spring from Jesus. After all, Jesus tells His disciples that the world will know they are His followers by their love. *"This is how all will know that you are my disciples, if you have love for one another."* (John 13:35)

Clearly, love is important. Love gives life. Love sustains life. And when we are at our best, love defines life.

How can we have this kind of love in our lives?

You Are a Child Loved by God

The Bible is a story of love: God's love for the world and God's love for His children. After all, God is love (1 John 4:8). Nowhere do we see the love of God more active than in Jesus. *"For God so loved the world that he gave his only Son, so that everyone who believes in him might not perish but might have eternal life."* (John 3:16)

This famous verse captures the heart of the Bible, the heart of the faith, and truly the heart of God. Jesus came to us because God loves us. That is the supreme example of agape love. God loves us first. God takes the first step. And the birth of Jesus proves that.

In Jesus, we see God taking the first step to touch and shape our lives. In offering His son to you, God shows you His highest dreams for your life. He wants us to be like Christ. *That* is the-best-version-of-yourself. Just as Jell-O takes the form of the container it is surrounded by, so too are we shaped by what we are surrounded by. God desires to immerse you in Himself, Jesus. In Him, you can fulfill God's dream for your life.

Jesus represents all that we humans can be. You are made in His image. As you become the-best-version-of-yourself, you become more and more like Jesus. Most of all, because He is willing to sacrifice Himself for us at the cross, Jesus represents love. That's what agape love is: self sacrificial love. Agape love means thinking of the other person first and being willing to sacrifice in order to help that person.

Jesus is God's agape love. God sent His son to us and then sacrificed Him for us. God loves you so much that He is willing to sacrifice His very own substance, Jesus, His son, on your behalf. That is the model of love. God loves us first.

Next, Jesus issues the invitation to us all: Love Him. Hear the words of Jesus: *"Whoever has my commandments and observes them is the one who **loves** me. And whoever **loves** me will be **loved** by my Father, and I will **love** him and reveal myself to him."* (John 14: 21) When we worship Jesus in the Eucharist, we love Him. When we obey Jesus and fulfill His commandments, we love Him. Our actions and our service to Him become expressions of our love for

Him. And when we love Jesus, we love God.

God loves us first. We then love Him in return. And the news gets even better! When we love Jesus, God in turn loves us and continues to show Himself to us even more. The relationship grows and strengthens. This is where our strength comes from: God's love flows into our lives and provides us with a special power that is unavailable in the world outside of Him. When we love Jesus, we come to know who we are. God's love becomes a part of who we are. Only then do we begin to realize the full potential that God has in mind for us. We start to understand *who* we are. And we also realize *whose* we are. We are God's children. We belong to God.

As God's children, and as lovers and followers of Jesus, we are invited to live in that love. *"As the Father loves me, so I also love you. Remain in my love."* (John 15:9) Jesus invites us to spend our days and our energies in that love. Love becomes not merely something we feel, or something we receive; love becomes where we live. We live in God's love. In fact, He is our dwelling place (Ps. 90:1). That is the most special gift of all. Jesus ushers us into a new life of love with Him and the Father above.

Self help books and self esteem courses can never replace the most basic fact that we belong to God. Only God can heal the human heart. God loves you. That is who you are: His precious child. God has dreams for your life. God has a blueprint for who He intends you to be. That blueprint gives your life meaning, direction, and purpose. And that God given dream begins with a simple word: love.

Who are you? *A child loved by God.*

Vertical Love

If Jesus had only one word in His vocabulary, it would be love. In fact, Jesus says all of His teaching can be summarized in that one powerful word: agape. When asked what the greatest teaching or commandment was, Jesus responded, *"Love God completely. And love your neighbor as yourself."* (Matthew 22:34–40)

The critical role of agape love can best be seen in Jesus's teaching in Mark 12. Perhaps paradoxically, this chapter of Mark shows the many ways in which Jesus disagreed with the Jewish leaders of His time. It is important to remember that Jesus was not always popular. In fact, He often found Himself mired in controversy. Some people loved to fight with Jesus or argue with Him. For example, in the Gospel of Mark alone, religious authorities, demons, Satan himself, and even occasionally Jesus's own disciples oppose Jesus and/or His teachings.

Therefore, it should not be surprising to open Mark's chapter 12 and find Jesus in the middle of a series of arguments. One disagreement leads directly to another. All kinds of people—chief priests, scribes, elders, Pharisees, Herodians, and Sadducees—parade through chapter 12 quibbling and arguing with Jesus over various matters. First, in Mark 12:1–12, Jesus tells the parable of the wicked tenants in the vineyard, and the religious authorities realize that He *"told this parable against them"* (12:12) in order to criticize their failure to serve God with their lives. In 12:13–17, Jesus avoids the trap that the authorities seek to set for Him regarding the issue of the payment of taxes. Sadducees question Jesus regarding the resurrection in 12:18–27, and Jesus denounces the scribes' ostentatious lifestyles in 12:38–40. He reinforces that denunciation with His observation of the supreme value of the widow's offering of a mite in 12:41–44.

However, it's easy to miss the point of this entire chapter. Unlike all the disputes in the rest of the chapter, in 12:28–34, Jesus and a scribe actually agree. Mark nestles this passage of agreement right between the first three disputes of chapter 12 and the final three disputes. In other words, the passage of agreement between Jesus and the religious authorities is located right at the center of chapter 12. This is the heart of the chapter, the centerpiece. The six stories of disagreement and debate only serve to highlight the focal point of the chapter: 12:28–34. This is the center of the chapter and the center of what binds believers together.

Well, then, on what do Jesus and the scribe agree? Love. That's it. They both agree that love is the centerpiece of becoming the-best-version-of-yourself. Love is the fulcrum.

When the scribe asks what the most important commandment of all is, Jesus responds with His famous call to love God entirely with all your heart, soul, mind, and strength as well as to love your neighbor as yourself. Rather than disagreeing with Jesus, the scribe quickly responds, *"You are right."* (12:32) Unlike all the other people portrayed in Mark 12, the scribe actually agrees with Jesus. Rather than no, he says yes.

Why does the scribe agree? Because Jesus perfectly captures the message of the Old Testament. Jesus's answer expands on the basic teachings found in Leviticus 19 and Deuteronomy 6. God's people are called to love God and love one another. What do the scribe and Jesus agree on? In a word, love.

The Old Testament and the New Testament converge in that one word: *agape*. Love that sacrifices self in order to love God with abandon. Love that gives in order to love your neighbors with joy. In contrast to all the conflicts in chapter 12 stands the central idea of love. Agape love.

In order to understand what Jesus is saying, it is important to remember that there were at least three basic kinds of love expressed in the Greek language. Knowing the difference helps us to know how to love God in our lives. Agape love is not brotherly love, like we feel for our families and friends. Nor is it erotic love, like that between husband and wife. Rather, agape love is self sacrificial love. Love that gives. Love that considers others first. Generous love. Self-giving love.

Agape is not a word that Mark throws around lightly in his Gospel. In fact, he uses this specific term only a few times. He uses it carefully, because in his mind, God and Jesus are the examples of agape. We find the models for how we are to love not in other human beings but in God and Jesus.

Jesus teaches us that agape love is vertical. Love moves up and down. God's love flows down from above and into your life. Love comes from God to you. The most significant example of that is in Jesus Himself. Jesus stepped out of heaven and came to you. God became flesh and lived among us (John 1:13–14). At Jesus's baptism (1:9–11) and at His transfiguration on the mountaintop (9:2–8), Jesus is God's "much-loved" son, the one for whom God the Father has agape love. Love that gives one's own son. Hear the words of God the Father: *"This is my Beloved Son."*

Mark explicitly shows that when Jesus meets the rich young ruler (10:17–22), He *"loves"* the ruler before He says, *"You are lacking in one thing. Go, sell what you have, and give to the poor."* (10:21) Love considers the needs of others first and foremost. Jesus loves the young ruler enough to tell him the truth. More importantly, He loves him enough to invite him to take steps to become the-best-version-of-himself.

When Jesus tells the parable of the wicked tenants in the vineyard, the Master (God the Father) sends His "beloved son" (Jesus) into the vineyard only to have the son rejected and killed by the tenants. This is self-sacrificial love, love that is willing to suffer on behalf of others. So, when Jesus calls you to lead a life of agape love, He is inviting you to imitate the divine example of love seen in God the Father and Jesus the Son. God loves you first. And He loves you sacrificially.

God has agape love for Jesus just as Jesus has agape love for you. The Trinity expresses the love of God in relationship. God, out of love, sends His beloved son and offers Him to you. He then imbues you with the Holy Spirit to give you power on your own journey. Agape is not part of the point; it is the point. Love forms the centerpiece of your relationship with God. God offers His own son, even to death. The cross stands out as the ultimate example of self giving, self-sacrificing love. The cross is love.

God loves you first. Best of all, He has always loved you. And His love flows generously down from above. Vertical love that saturates your life.

All you need is love: God's love.

Horizontal Love

Rainwater fills a birdbath from above. When the birdbath fills to capacity, it overflows and spills its contents on the ground. In contrast, a sprinkler receives its water from pipes and then liberally distributes that water all around. Better still, the sprinkler can be strategically positioned to water exactly the plants or areas the owner desires. And it can be moved to other dry areas when it is needed.

God's love operates just like rainwater. If you try to hold on to all the love that flows from above, you become like the birdbath. You cannot hold it all, so it just spills out haphazardly. In fact, you are in danger of becoming self-righteous as you hoard God's love in your life and fail to notice the people around you. The-best-version-of-yourself operates more like a sprinkler. You receive the love of God abundantly, and then you share it generously in the areas and with the people around you who need it most. In that way, God's vertical love becomes horizontal.

The point is simple: That same love that flows down from God and into your life shows up and gets expressed in how you treat other people. Because God has first loved you, He calls you to imitate that love and share it. That is horizontal love. Love is vertical as we love God above us and He loves us. Love is horizontal as God's divine love moves from us into the lives of real people. We are conduits of God's love to other people. You were made to be a sprinkler.

Having agape love in your life means that you will live differently from the rest of the world. "Jesus people" are different. Jesus captures that difference between God's people and the rest of the world in Luke 10:25–37, His famous parable of the Good Samaritan. You remember the story. A lawyer asks Jesus, *"What must I do to inherit eternal life?"* Jesus helps the man answer his own question in the same way Jesus Himself answers the scribe in the story we just looked at in Mark 12: with a call to love God and to love people. But then the scribe asks, *"And who is my neighbor?"* In other words, what does agape love look like in real life? Agape love is not just an idea. It can be seen and touched in the world we live in. Agape love requires a decision and an action.

Thus, Jesus shares the marvelous story of the man traveling from Jerusalem to Jericho on a Roman road when he is robbed, stripped, beaten, and left for dead alongside the road. A priest travels that way, sees the man, and passes by him on the other side of the road. A Levite holy man does the same thing. However, in a shocking surprise, a Samaritan, an outcast and an alien in the eyes of the Jews, is *"moved with pity"* (10:32) and stops to assist the victim. He bandages the man's wounds, anoints him with oil and wine for the healing of those wounds, and transports the man to an inn, where he offers to pay for the man's care and recovery. In other words, unlike the two Jewish leaders, the Samaritan gets off his donkey and does something. That is love.

Jesus then asks the scribe, *"Which of these three men was a neighbor to the man?"* The scribe responds, *"The one who showed mercy."* Then Jesus challenges him to *"Go and do likewise."* Go. Do. Love.

Jesus's point is clear: To have the agape love of God flowing in your life means that you will show mercy for other people. Why? Not because you are a good person. No. It is because we are God's people! We love because God first loves us. We show mercy because God first has shown mercy to us. We have agape love in our lives only because God has shown His love for us in Jesus. God invites you to share that love generously with the world. You do not act on your own. You act as God's beloved child, sharing God's love with a hurting world. Just as God in Himself shares His son in your life. God is love. And the-best-version-of-yourself will be too.

To share the love of God, or to have agape love flowing in your life, means that you are willing to inconvenience yourself on behalf of other people. You are willing to sacrifice self for the benefit of others. Just as God has offered Himself as a sacrifice for His children, you offer yourself to God and to His people. Agape love is costly. Loving others will cost you something. The Samaritan sacrificed his schedule, shared his donkey and wine, and paid the innkeeper with a promise to cover any additional costs needed to help the beaten man recover.

Love may mean that you give more money away to serve the needs of others than you spend on your own needs. It may mean a lunch hour spent in the hospital cradling and rocking a newborn child whose mother is unable to care for the baby's needs. It may mean an afternoon spent visiting a nursing home when we would really rather be playing golf. It may mean spending a vacation working on a mission team building a church in Honduras rather than surfing in Hawaii. It may mean praying with children in a classroom, or surrendering a prized seat to someone less able. Agape love is costly.

Agape love takes the initiative. It is active. Love does not wait for an invitation or a free moment. Love does not say, "I will do this when I retire," or "I hope to get around to that someday." Jesus Christ came into the world to die for our sins while we were still sinners. He did not wait until we asked for help. He did not procrastinate until it was a more convenient time for God. Love acts. As Jesus says, "Go and do. . . ."

A great Christian was asked how the Christian should live, and he responded, "Do all the good you can." Love does. Love acts. Love takes the initiative to benefit others. Love finds needs and ministers to them. Why? Because God sends us out into the world to be different. You are sharing God's own agape love in all that you say and do. No nobler purpose for life exists. And nothing else can satisfy your soul.

A good question to ask yourself is: How much love is evidenced in my life? At the end of this chapter, I will share with you five ways you can cultivate love as a bigger part of your life. Then you will be well on your way to becoming the-best-version-of-yourself.

Your Destiny in Love

One last thing about Jesus. He not only said that you are called to love God with abandon—with all your heart, all your mind, all your soul, and all your strength. He also invited you to love your neighbors with joy.

However, Jesus raised the bar even higher. In Matthew 5:43–48, He calls us to love our enemies. Listen to the words of Jesus: *"Love your enemies and pray for those who persecute you, that you may be children of your heavenly Father."* (5:44–45a)

Loving your enemies? Why? Because you want to be more like Jesus. God loves each human being. After all, every person is made in His image. God loves even those who do not love Him in return. He still seeks them. God never fails to extend His heart to them even when He is rejected. Those who follow Jesus begin to look more like Jesus and less like the world. In the world, we all love our friends and people who love us. That is the easy part. Few of us love our enemies or even pray for them.

However, when you begin to apply what Jesus teaches, you learn remarkable lessons. When you pray for those who hate you or persecute you, your own prayers begin to change you. Of course, your prayers also begin to change your enemies. But the great miracles occur as your own heart changes. You develop a greater capacity to love, even learning to love those who do not return your love. This is loving as God loves.

As these changes occur, you begin to become more and more like God. God is love (1 John 4:16). And love defines the-best-version-of-yourself. When God's love lives in us, it also is *"perfected in us."* (1 John 4:12) He perfects us as we grow in love. Think about that. God is making you perfect, through love.

As we grow in love, we grow in holiness. As we grow in holiness, we begin to become the very people that God intends us to be. His blueprint for our lives becomes a reality. *"For this is the will of God, your holiness . . ."* (1 Thess. 4:3). Over time, you become a person of holy love, sharing yourself, your resources, and the love of God with all of the world. You become the-best-version-of-yourself, God's dream for you.

Jesus makes quite a claim. God is at work in you to make you more like Jesus. In fact, Jesus is so bold as to challenge you: *"Be perfect, just as your heavenly Father is perfect."* (Matthew 5:48) Those are strong words. God's dream for you is perfection—not perfection in math or in basketball, but perfection in agape love. That is your destiny.

God desires that your heart resemble the heart of Jesus. And it pleases God when your actions, even including the loving of your enemies, look like the actions of Jesus. He wants you to act like Jesus did. Even more, He wants your motives to be like those of Jesus. Motives that are based in love. Motives that love God and love people.

Jesus invites you to a life full of love. Enjoy!

CULTIVATING A LIFE OF LOVE

1. Make a list of your enemies by name. Begin to pray daily for each name on your list. It may be easier to pray first for those with whom you still have a relationship. Then move on to the ones who trouble you most.

2. Serve a person who cannot possibly benefit you in return. Take some time one day a week to visit a resident at a nursing home, cuddle a newborn in need at the hospital, or do yard work for a disabled person.

3. Participate on a mission team with your church to serve people in severe poverty or crisis. Help rebuild an area after flood damage. Help build a church in a new community or foreign country. Lead a Vacation Bible School for children in a place where there is a great need. Learn to love by sacrificing your time and your money. Give your heart away and watch as God honors that by enlarging your heart.

4. Attend Mass more than one time per week and seek to love God more fully with your heart. Perhaps attend worship with a friend at a congregation unfamiliar to you to be stretched in a new way in your vertical love for God.

5. Give sacrificially. Anyone can give out of abundance. Make a gift to a scholarship fund, a children's home, or a hospice that is over and beyond your ordinary giving to God's Kingdom work. Feel the pinch of doing without something so that others might benefit from your sacrifice. Give thanks to Jesus, who sacrificed Himself for you without hesitation. Love God and love people at the same time.

JOY

"... the fruit of the Spirit is love, JOY, peace, patience, kindness, generosity, faithfulness, gentleness, self-control ..." Galatians 5:22–23

2. YOUR MOST ATTRACTIVE QUALITY
Come, share your master's joy.

Joy is surprisingly scarce these days. Technology makes you ever busier, and the frenzy around you increases. Joy is often the first thing to get squeezed out of your life. That's because joy finds it difficult to grow where stress is abundant. Stress chokes off joy like weeds choke off the growth of plants in your garden.

Even worse, pessimism and negativism kill joy. Scientists have even proved that your joy can be extinguished by negative people. Researchers studied the habits and lives of unhealthy families. Discovery: Negative fathers and husbands breed negative wives. Moreover, negative parents breed negative children. In other words, negativism is contagious—so contagious that your children can be swept up in its tidal wave if you are not careful.

How many miserable people have you known? Did you notice how negative people always found and surrounded themselves with other negative people? Did you notice how, when forced to interact with joyful people, the negative people tried to persuade and discourage the more positive people around them? Negativism breeds negativism. It is not difficult to find people to tell you why things won't work out like you hope and plan. It is easy to find people to rain on your parade. Most negative people are more than willing to share their dark thoughts and worries with you. In fact, they often can't wait for the opportunity.

These same researchers also discovered that while negativism is highly contagious, joy is not so contagious. Joyful husbands do not necessarily help foster joyful wives. Nor do joyful parents always produce joyful children. Joy is not passed on as easily as negativism. Joy must be cultivated. Joy requires effort. Joy can be hard work.

However, the apostle Paul reminds us that joy is at the center of the Christian's life. We are Easter people. Christ has defeated death. God has vanquished Satan. Easter has conquered Good Friday. That means we are people of joy. That is how Saint Paul, writing from a Roman prison, a difficult circumstance that would cause most people to lose hope, writes to the Christians in the church at Philippi, "*Rejoice in the Lord always. I shall say it again: rejoice!*" (Phil. 4:4). Roman prisons were dark, dank places of death. Most prisoners died there. Yet, Paul found joy in his imprisonment.

In fact, in a letter from prison to the Philippians, rather than writing of his sufferings and worries, Paul mentions his "joy in Christ" more than twelve times in just four chapters. That is worth hearing: Even in the most difficult times in your life, you can rely upon the deep, abiding joy that comes from Jesus Christ. The world and your circumstances may press in and seek to crush you, but a relationship with Jesus will grow a joy in you that cannot be squelched.

Joy lives at the very center of Christian life. Joy makes us Christians different. We do not despair; we rejoice. Even when the world is closing in, we still have joy. Why? Three reasons: the simple joy of discovering Jesus, the deep joy of living in Jesus, and the eternal joy of dying in Jesus.

The Simple Joy of Discovering Jesus

The angel told us to expect joy, remember? On an ordinary night, the shepherds were gathered out in the fields, minding their own business and tending to their flocks. And then the angel of the Lord stood before them and the glory of the Lord shone around them. Can you imagine? Imagine being at work one evening only to have the glory of the Lord show up right in front of you. Wow!

Then the angel speaks: *"Do not be afraid; for, behold, I proclaim to you good news of great JOY that will be for all the people."* (Luke 2:10) Jesus, God's son and our Savior, has been born in Bethlehem. Great joy! For all people. The angel knew from the very beginning: Jesus's arrival in the world brings joy. So too does His arrival in your heart and in your life. With Jesus living in you, unspeakable joy takes root. The very same joy that the angel shared with the shepherds on Christmas evening.

The wise men knew it too. They followed a star all the way from the East. These men traveled a great distance, having no idea where the star would guide them, and made their way to a little village called Bethlehem. *"They were overjoyed at seeing the star."* (Matthew 2:10) The wise men's search culminated in a stable in a little village that few people even knew about. Their journey ended with the overwhelming discovery of the arrival of Jesus, born in a manger. Overwhelmed with joy.

Are you beginning to get the picture? *Jesus brings joy.* He brought joy even when He was a newborn. He brings joy now to those who love Him. His joy is contagious. The truth cannot be avoided: Christians have joy.

Jesus even taught His followers that to know God is to have abundant, unspeakable joy:

"The kingdom of heaven is like treasure buried in a field, which a person finds and hides again, and out of joy goes and sells all that he has and buys that field." (Matthew 13:44)

The joy of discovering Jesus and the Kingdom of God surpasses anything else that you will ever know in this lifetime.
Consider the joy you feel when you find money on the sidewalk.
Or when you are out of town and unexpectedly run into someone
you know. Or when you have lost a piece of jewelry and then find
it. It is amazing how much joy we gain in finding and discovering something.

Yet, the joy of meeting Jesus for the first time and gaining
entry into a new way of life exceeds the joy of everything else.
There is no joy like that of being part of the Kingdom of God.
Incomprehensible joy. Divine joy. Unswerving joy. That is Jesus
joy! Jesus is no mere theory or story. Either He is the source of
incomparable joy or He is nothing at all.

The Deep Joy of Living in Jesus

The great joy that Jesus brings to you when you first meet Him
only serves to prepare you for the increasing joy you will experience in your journey. You are now a part of the Resurrection, an
Easter person. You belong to God and are now free to live your
life the way God intended, toward becoming the-best-version-of-
yourself. You are set free from seeking to please others or desperately trying to satisfy yourself and can now please and serve the
Lord. You are free from the heavy weight of the demands of the
world upon you. Free to be the person that God designed you to
be from the very beginning.

This immense joy and freedom is made possible because of
the empty tomb. Jesus put sin to death once and for all. He gained
victory over the forces of Satan and evil in the world when He
died at Calvary.

But His death was not the end. Rather, it was only the beginning. Early in the morning, Mary Magdalene and the other Mary

went to the tomb to see Jesus's body one more time. They hoped to anoint his body with oil. These ladies probably intended to pray and spend time with God as they grieved the death of their very special friend, Jesus. But when they arrived at the tomb, an earthquake shook the ground, and an angel appeared. Just as the angel had spoken to the shepherds, the angel now spoke to the two Marys: "Do not be afraid! I know that you are seeking Jesus the crucified. He is not here, for he has been raised just as he said. . . ." (Matthew 28:5–6)

What did Mary and Mary do with this shocking news that Jesus was not in the tomb? How did they react to an earthquake and the arrival of an angel who shared with them that Jesus had in fact been raised from the dead? They left quickly with *"fear and* **great joy***."* (Matthew 28:8) Mary and Mary were the very first to know that the Resurrection was real. It was not just some bold prediction by Jesus. As they left the tomb and the angel that Easter morning, they ran squarely into Jesus Himself, raised from the dead. No wonder they had fear (Who has seen a resurrected man?) and great joy (Jesus lives!).

The two Marys had joy because they knew. They knew that Jesus had not been a madman who only claimed to be able to conquer death. Mary and Mary knew that Jesus lives. They discovered that God is indeed bigger than life and bigger than death. They realized that death does not have the last word in your life. They found that Jesus was exactly who He said He was: the Son of God. He has prepared a place for us. He does intend to take us to be with God for eternity. He is the very Word of God made flesh. *That* is unspeakable joy.

And that joy changes how you live. It is indeed a life-changing experience to live with the knowledge that God has a plan for you, and His plans extend even beyond the grave. You are a spiritual person, not merely a physical person with an earthly body. We humans are more than bodies or sophisticated animals. There is a whole spiritual realm that we cannot see or touch with our hands. We are not confined by this world or its values. We have become a part of God's world. Jesus has expanded your view of the universe beyond the here and now—indeed, beyond the grave. Now, that is joy!

Joy is just what Jesus intends for you. It is His goal that joy will be a vital part of your life. Hear His words: *"I have told you this so that* **my joy may be in you and your joy may be complete.***"* (John 15:11) Jesus comes to bring you the joy of God. Becoming the-best-version-of-yourself may involve some struggle and pain, but it will most certainly be defined by joy. Why? Because you are doing exactly what the Lord of the Universe intends for you. Better still, He introduces you to the Holy Spirit, who completes you and makes you whole on the journey. Knowing God the Father, God the Son in Jesus, and God the Holy Spirit completes you with a divine joy. This is why you are here. To be in relationship with the One who made you, He who loves you, and He who will sustain you to the very end and beyond. The world may offer brief moments of happiness here and there, but it cannot offer deep, real joy.

Possessing that joy helps you to endure whatever life may bring. The writer of Hebrews shares how early Christians faced suffering, trials, abuses, persecution, the theft of their posses- sions, and even imprisonment. How could they weather these vi- olent storms? They had a *"better and lasting possession."* (Hebrews 10:34) They possessed salvation and life in Jesus Christ, which produces a joy in living that does not succumb to the world. A deep joy that cannot be extinguished by the hardships of the world or even by suffering. Jesus Joy is eternal and powerful.

You may not be able to see and touch that spiritual world, but you belong to it now nonetheless. Hear the words of Saint Peter:

Although you have not seen Him, you love him.

Even though you do not see Him now yet believe in him

you rejoice with an indescribable and glorious joy,

as you attain the goal of your faith,

the salvation of your souls. (1 Peter 1:8–9)

Knowing that "glorious joy" frees you to live joyfully. You can thank those who criticize you. You can bless those who curse you. You can love those who hate you. Why? Because you have a joy that cannot be squelched or extinguished. That joy changes you. It changes the way you live. It changes you forever.

The Rev. Hosea Williams worked alongside Dr. Martin Luther King Jr. during the civil rights movement in America in the 1960s. In fact, Williams was with Dr. King when King was assassinated in Memphis, Tennessee, by James Earl Ray. In an interview, Williams describes how he felt when he saw Dr. King lying on the motel walkway, bleeding to death from the gunshot wound. "I wanted to go out and get a gun and kill the first white people I saw," he says. But he changed his mind before he acted, "because Martin had taught me differently."

Even in times of violence and immense suffering, that indescribable joy of Jesus allows believers to live differently from the world. As a believer, you will see the world differently. You belong to God and to Jesus now. You walk in the Spirit of God. Your values are different from the world's values. You can love and bless even when you are hated and cursed.

Oh, the joy! The deep joy of living in Jesus.

The Joy of Dying in Jesus

My favorite teaching of Jesus is the parable of the talents in Matthew 25:14–30. This is the greatest story Jesus shared about how

God wants you to live. Remember the details. A wealthy man, going on a journey, calls together his servants and entrusts his property to them while he will be away. To one servant the man gives five talents (a huge sum of money: about two million dollars today), to another servant he gives two talents, and to the third servant one talent. The first two servants go off to invest and trade the money entrusted to them in order to generate a return on investment for their master. The third servant, however, is afraid of losing the money he received. Rather than risking a loss in investing, he digs a hole in the ground and buries the money there.

When the master returns, he calls his servants together to hear about their activity and the management of his assets while he was away. The first two servants display the results of their work on his behalf. They have both doubled the sums of money that the master entrusted to them. Hear how the master greets and congratulates these two faithful servants: *"Well done, my good and faithful servant. Since you were faithful in small matters, I will give you great responsibilities. Come, share your master's joy."* (Matthew 25:21, 23)

In other words, when the master finds that his servants have taken risks and served him in order to produce results, he greets them with joy.

In contrast, the third servant shares how he buried the money in the ground because he was scared of making a mistake or losing it. He receives neither congratulations nor a reward. Instead, the master issues a rebuke for the third servant's unwillingness to take risks or to work on behalf of his master. Jesus labels that third servant lazy, and the master casts him out of the kingdom altogether. That is anything but joy.

Jesus's point seems clear. God entrusts each of us with many things, including financial assets as well as individual gifts and graces. His investment in you may differ from His investment in another person, but His investment in you is undeniable. Your life, your health, your body, your family, your innate talents, your education, your money, your passions, and your dreams—these are the materials God entrusts to you as you cooperate with Him to become the-best-version-of-yourself. Moreover, God blesses you with the presence and the power of the Holy Spirit. That is some kind of investment on God's part. And God expects and desires a return on that investment. God designed you to work in and for His Kingdom. He invites you to live your life so that you share not only your gifts with Him and the world but also, in the end, His joy.

When you serve God faithfully and bear fruit in your life, God welcomes you into His eternal joy. Can you envision the joy of entering heaven knowing that you have been faithful with your life and with God's call to work for Him? *"Come, share your master's joy."* No other words can compare with that now or eternally. How does one possibly measure the joy of being a part of the Kingdom of God, of living with God forever?

If you have been in the room with someone who is dying, you know there is a mammoth difference between those who die in Christ and those who do not. When a person dies in Christ, there is a deep, eternal peace and joy. Such people move gently into the next life, calm with the assurance of Jesus's promise of eternal joy. They find peace with their families and peace with themselves. In death, that peace brings joy.

Other people, however, die in turbulence, struggling and fighting with themselves, with family members, and with God to the bitter end. Joy is strangely absent in these deaths. Instead, there is merely tension and unrest.

So, in the end, there is a joy of dying in Jesus. When God's

Easter people die, we know that He meets us and prepares to usher us into His presence. Jesus has prepared a place for us after death. He has been raised, and so shall you. The joy you experience now as you live in Christ is but the first fruit of the joy you will share then.

Oh, the joy of Christ. Christ in life. Christ in death. And Christ for eternity.

GROWING A LIFE OF JOY

1. Find a joy mentor. There is no better way to grow in joy than to be around people who have it. Select a person in your life who has an abundant amount of joy. Spend time with him or her on a regular basis. This time helps to offset the effect that the negative people in your life may have on you. Let this joyful person teach you habits and routines from his or her own life that lead to increased joy. Notice where joyful people spend their time and what kinds of things they do, and identify the sources of their joy. Learn to imitate those habits and routines.

2. Pick your friends and settings. People who participate in Alcoholics Anonymous know that in order to beat alcoholism, an addict must change his or her playgrounds and playmates. An alcoholic simply cannot continue to hang around in the same places and with the same people as before. So too if you want to find joy. Actively seek to be in environments that cultivate your joy. Avoid settings and people who carp and criticize ceaselessly. Their negative outlooks will wear you down. Instead, surround yourself as often as possible with joyful people. Spend your time in places that encourage your own joyfulness. Remember the lesson that negative people breed negative people. Remove yourself as often as possible from such influences. This simple decision will have a dramatic impact on your life.

3. Endow your children with joy. Remember that negative, unhealthy behaviors in families are contagious and are usually passed down from one generation to the next. Christians have an awesome responsibility to pass on the joy of Christ to their own children. *"I have no greater joy than this, to hear that my children are walking in the truth."* (3 John 4) What brings your children joy? Spending time with you? Reading together? Playing games? Then do it. Introduce them to your own joy by praying with them, worshipping with them, and sharing the faith with them. Your children will learn joy by imitating you. Soon you will discover that your own joy begins to increase simply by absorbing the joy of your children.

4. Make a thanksgiving list. Each day for a week, in your prayer life, list specific things in your life for which you are thankful. These are some of your joys. Don't be general (e.g., life, wealth, family). Be specific. Name your joys one by one. For example, baseball, barbecue, bluegrass music, your priest, a faithful friend or your spouse, a colleague at work, etc. Give thanks to God in prayer for these joys of your life. As you pay more attention to these joys by listing them and thanking God for them, you will begin to notice other things that give you joy. The more you notice, the more you will be able to cultivate the parts of your life that grow your joy.

5. Get a Mass journal and use it. Take the journal with you each Sunday when you go to Mass. Write down the one thing that God says to you in that experience and reread it each day throughout the week. The Mass highlights the wonderful intimacy we have with Jesus as He gives us His own body and blood in the Eucharist. Use the Mass journal to focus your attention on Jesus's sacrifice and seeking the presence of the Holy Spirit as you receive the elements. All of these lead to a deeper sense of joy in the Lord. The Eucharist is Jesus's special gift to His followers. Use it. Celebrate it!

PEACE

". . . the fruit of the Spirit is love, joy, PEACE, patience, kindness, generosity, faithfulness, gentleness, self-control . . ." Galatians 5:22–23

Peace

3. AVOIDING THE-WORST-VERSION-OF-YOURSELF

To understand what the-best-version-of-yourself looks like, it is also helpful to know what it does not look like: the-worst-version-of-yourself.

Pause for just a moment. Breathe peace in. Where do you need peace?

Lots of people talk about desiring world peace. But when you think about it, very few of us have peace even in our families or our homes, or perhaps even in our own souls. If there is no peace there in the smallest unit of living, how in the world can we hope for peace in the entire world?

In a church I attended years ago, the pastor ended each service with "prayers for peace." Slowly and surely, we prayed each week for peace in the different areas of our lives. We prayed for peace in our hearts, in our homes, in our streets, in our relationships, in our cities, in our nation, and in our world. In a remarkable way, we all began to notice just how little peace existed in our world. Those prayers for peace began to grow peace in the lives of our church members and in the city where we lived at the time.

Again, pause for just a moment. Meditate. Pray. Where do you need peace?

Unquestionably, peace is God's business. This study focuses

on the two powerful verses of Galatians 5:22–23, the fruit of the Spirit. Those two verses contain the keys to becoming the-best-version-of-yourself. However, to understand what the-best-version-of-yourself looks like, it is also helpful to know what it does not look like: the-worst-version-of-yourself.

For that look at the-worst-version-of-yourself, Saint Paul provides Galatians 5:19–21. He calls these verses the "works of the flesh." And notice how these works of the flesh come right before the fruit of the Spirit. In other words, Saint Paul wants you to see the contrast: Point, meet counterpoint.

Before the apostle Paul shows you the fruit that God's Spirit will bear in your life when you live in His Spirit, he displays for all to see exactly what the fleshly life, or life in the world, looks like. Fleshly, worldly living is the exact opposite of life in the Spirit.

The-worst-version-of-yourself is the exact opposite of the-best-version-of-yourself. Notice what he mentions as works of the flesh: *"immorality, impurity, licentiousness, idolatry, sorcery,* ***hatreds, rivalry, jealousy, outbursts of fury, acts of selfishness, dissensions, factions, occasions of envy,*** *drinking bouts, orgies, and the like . . . those who do such things will not inherit the Kingdom of God."*

Count them. Of the fifteen "works of the flesh" listed, eight are clearly related to the lack of peace in your relationships with other people. Those eight strifes or tensions are in boldface above: hatreds, rivalry, jealousy, outbursts of fury, acts of selfishness, dissensions, factions, occasions of envy. In all of these, peace is lacking. Where peace is absent, bickering and division abound.

The-worst-version-of-yourself means a life filled with strife, discord, and anger in all your relationships. Continual disharmony everywhere you turn. The-worst-version-of-yourself lacks peace, and Saint Paul makes it plain that that peace comes only from the Spirit. When you live and walk in the Spirit of God, His peace will saturate your life, even your difficult relationships.

The truth leaps from the words of these verses regarding the works of the flesh. God cares about your relationships with other people. God desires for you to be in a right relationship with Him as well as with your neighbors. When you live in the Spirit of God, you will soon discover peace sprouting up in your relationships. Anger and quarrels will begin to fade, and peace will begin to grow in their place. Jesus leads to peace.

Those are important words to hear. They are life-giving words. Hear them again: Jesus leads to peace. He leads nowhere else.

In homes where abuse and violence have taken root, Jesus leads to peace. In streets where gang members make the rules, Jesus leads to peace. In relationships broken by gossip or deception, Jesus leads to peace. In lives fractured by addictions or failures, Jesus leads to peace. In nations such as England, where rowdy, violent soccer fans triple the cost of security wherever they travel, or the United States, where the schools grow increasingly violent and dangerous, Jesus leads to peace.

Where there is turbulence and unrest, quiet and stillness are found only in the Lord Jesus. Life in the Spirit of God means peace.

And peace means three things: peace with God, peace with self, and then, peace with others.

Peace with God

Clearly, the first priority in your life is to find peace with God. Without that peace first, you will have no other peace. Achieving peace with God is the seed for growing the fruit of peace in the other parts of your life.

It is important to remember that peace is spiritual. It is not something that can be purchased or manufactured. It is not something that you can create for yourself or from within yourself. Peace comes from above; it comes from God. There is no other way.

It is a simple fact that God made us humans to be in a relationship with Him. There is a part of you that is made for God alone; a part of your soul is reserved for God. He has a significant place just for Himself in your life. There is no substitute for His presence there. When we choose to reject God, our souls are restless. When we exclude God from His rightful place in our lives, our lives are incomplete. Without God, we are without peace. That is how we are made. Saint Augustine said it this way: "Our hearts are restless until they rest in You, O Lord."

The Scriptures plainly show that peace is the work of Jesus. Just as the angel told the shepherds of a great joy in Bethlehem when Jesus was born, so too did the heavenly host sing to the shepherds of *"Peace on Earth."* (Luke 2:14) When Jesus rode on a donkey into the city of Jerusalem, as the people placed palms before Him, the crowds cried out to Him, *"Blessed is the King who comes in the name of the Lord. Peace in heaven and glory in the highest."* (Luke 19:38) As He entered, Jesus wept for the city and said, *"If you had only recognized the things that make for peace!"* Jesus not only brings peace; He makes peace. In fact, He is peace, the Prince of Peace. When He was born, the angels proclaimed it. As He prepared to die, He exuded it.

That is why Paul refers to the Gospel of Jesus as the *"Gospel of Peace."* (Eph. 6:15) In fact, Paul invites us to put on the armor of God to protect ourselves from the world and from the devil. The world is a violent, turbulent place. Terrorists prey on the innocent and unsuspecting. Sin lures us away from righteousness. The devil seeks to lead us away from God and preys on our weaknesses. We need protection. With the armor of God, we can fend off attack and resist temptation. In that armor described by Saint Paul, what is it that protects our feet? Answer: the Gospel of Peace. *"And with your feet fitted with the readiness that comes from the gospel of peace."*

Think about it for a moment. When we live in Jesus, we

acquire peace. A peace from God. A divine peace. However, that peace not only lives in you; it protects you. When temptation comes and produces its turbulence and disturbance, the devil tries to swirl you around, confuse you, and disorient you. That has happened so often in my own life that I can hardly share just one example. Time and time again, when I have decided to follow Jesus in a decision, the very next thing to happen is a piercing temptation from the devil seeking to move me away from that decision. The devil always tempts me. His temptation always confuses me. He always makes me wonder if I am really listening to God. The devil sows evil with confusion and unrest.

At those times, you can stand on the peace that God has given you. That is important to know because temptation and the wiles of the devil will shake you and create a restlessness within you that makes you doubt every one of your own steps. That shaking can be resisted only with a deep spiritual peace. A divine peace.

Romans 8:5–6 captures this point best: *"For those who live according to the flesh are concerned with the things of the flesh, but those who live according to the spirit with the things of the Spirit. The concern of the flesh is death,* **but the concern of the spirit is life and peace.***"*

When your heart and mind are set on the flesh and on the world, there is nothing but unrest and strife. There is no peace. Your heart is unsettled, and your relationships are too. But set your mind on the Spirit and on the things of God, and soon your heart finds peace and life itself.

Remember again the simple prayer of Saint Augustine: "Our hearts are restless until they rest in You, O Lord." You are made for God. Without Him, you are restless and turbulent. Without Him, your soul and heart will succumb to every temptation and every passion. You will be governed by your own whims and desires. You will love pleasure and live for the flesh. You will be unable to have peace with your neighbors because you have no peace in your own heart.

However, with God, you have a peace that can withstand anything. In fact, you have a peace that *"surpasses all understanding [and] will guard your hearts and minds in Christ Jesus."* (Phil. 4:7) That occurs when the fruit of peace grows in your life through the powerful presence of the Holy Spirit.

No one on earth can give you that kind of deep, spiritual peace. You cannot find it in a book or from deep within yourself. That peace can come only from our Maker, God. Before there is any other peace, you must first have peace with God.

If you do not have peace with God, stop right now and pray. Ask God to still your heart and your mind. Pray these words: "O Lord, how majestic is your name in all the earth. You created me out of nothing. You made me for your own pleasure and delight. Forgive me for living for myself. Thank you, Jesus, for forgiving my sins. Set me free to love you first in my life. Calm the storms stirring within my soul. Give me your peace. Come to me; live within me. Set me free, I pray. Amen."

Peace with Self

Once you have obtained peace with God, you will begin to see the fruit of peace growing in your life. Jesus gives you that peace. Hear His words: *"Peace I leave with you; my peace I give to you. Not as the world gives do I give it to you. Do not let your hearts be troubled or afraid."* (John 14:27)

Where life in the world once brought fear, anxiety, and unrest, Jesus now brings stillness and peace. He gives you a peace that you cannot obtain in the world. Once you knew only troubles and fears; now you know the Master of the Universe, Creator of All. You have found your purpose and your direction. Jesus is your peace. He lives in you, and His Spirit guides you. Release; you are free.

Peace with self means knowing who you are: a child of God.

Your value is not determined by the size of your savings account. You are not merely your job or what you do. You are more than your father's son or daughter. You belong to Jesus. He guides your life. He prepares your way. You are at peace with yourself.

Again, hear the words of Jesus: *"I have told you this so that you might have* **peace** *in me. In the world you will have trouble, but take courage, I have conquered the world."* (John 16:33)

Once you have peace within yourself, the world and its powers no longer rule over you. Even persecution and suffering can be endured, because your peace is not based on health, or rank, or your income. Your peace lives within you, and His name is Jesus. Remember those words from the beginning of this study: *". . . yet I live, no longer I, but Christ lives in me."* Jesus is the living embodiment of peace within you.

Jesus has conquered the world. He invites you to follow Him to the same victory. You can now live the life God wants you to have. You are free from the demands of the world. You no longer have to please other people first. You live to please God, not man. That is peace. You know who you are. You are an Easter person.

The best picture of this peace comes in John 20:19–22. After Jesus has died, His disciples gather together in a house. They lock the doors out of fear. They no longer have their leader, Jesus. They fear what the world might do to them. They fear for the future. What happened to God's son? What happened to God's future? And where do they go now?

In the middle of their fear, Jesus appears in the center of the room. He stands before them. What does He say? *"**Peace** be with you."*

The disciples are crippled by fear. Jesus says, *"Peace."*

His followers are bewildered and spiritually lost. Jesus says, *"Peace."*

After He shows them His hands and His side, with their nail holes from the cross, Jesus says again, *"Peace be with you."* Then He breathes on them and says, *"Receive the Holy Spirit."*

When His followers are lost, Jesus brings peace. When they feel alone, Jesus reminds them that He is there. He breathes on them and gives them the Holy Spirit.

Jesus has already breathed on you. You are a baptized follower of Jesus. Feel His breath wash over you. Live in that knowledge and that power. Accept His peace. Jesus offers it to you. Accept it. *"Peace be with you."* Live in peace.

Peace with God + Peace with Self = Peace with Others

Have you ever met someone who was always quarreling? Always fighting with others, bickering, complaining, gossiping, criticizing? Wherever he or she went, dissension went along and prospered. That person has no peace with others because he has no peace within himself.

Until you have peace with God, you cannot have peace within yourself. Until you have peace within yourself, you cannot possibly hope to have peace with other people. I cannot have peace with others if I do not know who I am in the first place.

This simple equation captures the flow of peace in your life:

Peace with God + Peace with Self = Peace with Others.

Peace flows in that sequence.

First, you must find and receive peace with God. You do that when you follow the lordship of Jesus in your life. That is when you begin to set your mind on the things of the Spirit. With that peace in hand, you then discover peace within. Again: "Our hearts are restless until they rest in You, O Lord."

From the divine peace of Jesus then begins to blossom the peace of God at work in your life. What does that look like? The Bible makes it plain:

Bless those who persecute you; bless and do not curse them.

Rejoice with those who rejoice, weep with those who weep.

Live in harmony with one another;

do not be haughty but associate with the lowly;

do not claim to be wiser than you are.

Do not repay anyone evil for evil, but take thought of what is noble in the sight of all.

If it is possible, so far as it depends on you, **live peaceably with all.**
(Romans 12:14–18 [NRSV])

Walking in the Spirit and desiring the fruit of peace in your life means that you live and behave peaceably. Revenge is removed from your motives and even from your vocabulary. Violence is rejected. Jesus has made a new path for you. As a result, your values are different from the world's. Where the world is violent and vengeful, Christians sow peace. The-best-version-of-yourself spreads peace wherever it goes.

The-best-version-of-yourself is not concerned with looking good in front of others. You no longer seek to impress or to grandstand. That creates unrest because it is false. You are who you are: a child of God moving to become the-best-version-of-yourself. That is enough. Pride is replaced with humility. Evil is repaid with good. Violence is answered with peace.

How can this be? What would make a person not seek revenge? Why would anyone refuse to brag and impress? In a word, peace. Peace with God. Peace with self. Peace with others.

It is a divine gift. Peace is a fruit of the Spirit.

Jesus breathes it. We live in it. The peace that surpasses all understanding.

GROWING A LIFE OF PEACE

1. Know His peace. Three times each day pause and remember the words of Jesus: *"My peace I give you."* Feel His breath wash over you as He breathes His peace and His Spirit on you. Bask in the warmth of His power and live in peace.

2. Develop a "psalm habit." The book of Psalms is full of every human emotion imaginable: fear, joy, sadness, confidence, despair, and elation. The psalms speak the very things we all wish we could say to God. If you read one psalm each day (or spend time on the same psalm every day for one week), the peace of God will grow in your soul. Read the psalms, pray the psalms, sing the psalms, study and meditate on the psalms, live in the psalms for a while. Allow them to breathe the peace-filled Word of God into your soul.

3. Confess your sins. Spend time each week in confession and self evaluation before God. Increase your frequency of using the Sacrament of Reconciliation. Prepare ahead of time by using an examination of conscience. Be honest with God and with yourself. Examine your heart for the areas that need God's cleansing touch. Share those with God and your priest. Invite God into every area of your life and mind and heart. As you do so, God's peace will replace the tension and restlessness within you.

4. Fast once day a month when you pray. Make fasting a part of your spiritual life. Feel free to consult a doctor before doing this if you have medical concerns. Begin small—fast for one meal. Grow into the ability to fast for twenty-four hours or more, always drinking liquids to avoid dehydration. Fasting helps to reveal the things that control you. Food is one of those things, but fasting also helps reveal your anger, your anxieties, and your lack of peace. Where does your unrest come from? What is blocking your ability to have peace in your heart and in your relationships? Fast when you pray. Pray that God will reveal the sources of your own lack of peace and set you free to have peace with Him and peace with others in your life.

5. Become an agent of peace. Write a letter of apology to someone you have hurt, even if he is a despicable person or she is a gossip. Share your heart so that God's peace might flow in you and through you.

PATIENCE

"... the fruit of the Spirit is love, joy, peace, PATIENCE, kindness, generosity, faithfulness, gentleness, self-control ..." Galatians 5:22–23

4. HOW YOU KNOW
YOU ARE MATURE

*The Spirit makes Himself known to us as we
learn to experience the hand of God in our suffering
rather than in spite of our suffering.*

Patience is a virtue. Or so they tell me.

More unfortunately, I am a classic type A personality, impatient and always wanting to get on to the next task on my to-do list. I am not proud of my impatience, but I am growing to recognize that patience will be a struggle in every strand of my DNA.

Sitting in traffic with a friend, after having waited in line twenty minutes to purchase tickets to a movie to be shown four hours later (because all the earlier showings were already sold out), we politely stopped short of a traffic light at the exit of the theater parking lot, in order to allow cars to pass in front of us to cross through to the other side of the lot.

This plan worked well for a minute or two. We waited patiently, proud of the Spirit's work in us, as the cars passed in front of us. The driver of each car seemed grateful for the break in the line of traffic, a logjam that had been preventing their progress.

This plan worked well for us, but evidently it was not so pleasing for the occupants of the car behind us. After a minute or two, they quickly swerved out of line and darted in front of us in line at the light, thereby cutting off the crossover traffic. All the other cars in the parking lot were logjammed once again.

Of course, the car that had bypassed us and cut everyone off had a Christian symbol fish sticker on the back. A moment earlier, I had been oh so proud of my level of patience; with this new intrusion of the impatient car in our path, my own patience went out the window and was quickly replaced with "road rage." All of a sudden, I felt like my entire world was under siege. The blood rushed to my head. My throat constricted. I ranted to my friend about the egregious act of the driver of the other car. My friend worked hard to calm me down and prevent my anger from outshining my impatience. Not a pretty scene.

However, somehow, God assures you (and me) that patience is a fruit of His Spirit. God intends for patience to grow within you as the Holy Spirit shapes your heart. God is patient, and He desires for His children to be patient too.

As a child in a worship service said, "Patience means you have to wait a lot." And the Scriptures have a lot to say about patience. In fact, the Bible describes three kinds of patience: end-time patience, social patience, and personal patience (or endurance).

End-time Patience

Believers wait for the Lord. That is a simple fact but an important one. Christians wait for the Lord. We wait for the coming of the Lord. We wait for the completion of the Lord's plans in the world. We wait for the return of Jesus. We wait for the arrival of the Kingdom of God. We wait for our souls to be united with Jesus forever. We wait for justice to be brought upon the evils of this world. We wait. That is end-time patience. All Christians live with an eye toward God's eternal future.

Of course, God works on His own time with His own ways. We, as humans, can merely wait and anticipate what God will do. It is comforting to know that God is already at work in the world and in your life right here and right now. But there is also a sense within each spirit that God is up to much more in the world than at first meets the human eye. God's ways are often mysterious, and humans can only wait to discern what He is up to.

God is at work carefully bringing about His Kingdom. He is working to bring all creation unto Himself. The Holy Spirit's work in each believer's heart is certainly a part of that greater work of God, but God is also about the cosmic business of completing creation and bringing everything to consummation. We humans can merely wait and anticipate. What a blessing that day will be when Jesus arrives for His children. When God ushers in His Kingdom once and for all. When evildoers are swept away and impurity is banished from the world. When we are restored to our eternal place near the throne of God to be joined with believers from all times and all places in singing the praises of our Lord and our God. What a day! Come, Lord Jesus, come.

Patience for "that day" is end-time patience. Christians already know the outcome of history. We know where we are headed. We know the ending already. We have the assurance of God's final victory. In the meantime, we wait and anticipate. End-time patience.

God wins. And that is good news. That final victory provides the singular focus of the book of Revelation: God wins in the end. Because you know that ending and you know your eternal destination, you can live differently than the world lives. You can possess a patience that the world does not have. Why? Because you know that the purpose of God will prevail in the end. Your citizenship is in heaven (Phil. 3:20). Therefore, you can live your life according to God's values.

You need not worry that you will not get enough things or fulfillment in this lifetime. You do not invest yourself completely in the achievements of this worldly life, for you know that there is a life to come that is more important and more rewarding.

Life with God is eternal. Knowing that fact makes patience much easier to grasp and to possess. You do not lose heart when things do not work out as you hoped, because you know there is coming a day when the purpose of God will prevail. Right will be made right, and evil will be no more. That is worth waiting for. Christians know that.

That is Kingdom patience. And that is end-time patience: knowing that God wins in the end. Knowing that you do not have to frantically go through this life trying to get all the goods and all the pleasure that you can. Instead, you are free to lead a patient life, serving God and anticipating the completion of His work in the world. You possess a patience that the world does not have. End-time patience.

Hebrews 6:9–12 (NRSV) expresses end-time patience this way:

Even though we speak in this way, beloved, we are confident of better things in your case, things that belong to salvation. For God is not unjust; He will not overlook your work and that love that you showed for His sake in serving the saints as you still do. And we want each one of you to show the same diligence so as to realize the full assurance of hope to the very end, so that you may not become sluggish but imitators of ***those who through faith and patience inherit the promises.***

This end-time patience grows in you as we grow in the Spirit. You indeed labor now, knowing that God will reward your labors in the end. Some rewards will come in the here and now; others will come later in the Kingdom. Nevertheless, God always rewards faithfulness.

Since we know without question that God rewards faithfulness, the Spirit can work patience in us. Our hearts can be put at rest when the rewards are not apparent right here and right now. Why? Because we know that God is faithful and will stand by us in the end. That is worth working for, and that is worth waiting for.

This kind of patience is beyond value, isn't it? The Holy Spirit provides a whole level of internal peace that allows you to live richer, fuller lives. You can afford to be patient because you know that this life is not the end but merely an anticipation of eternity with our Lord. You know that there is more to this life than meets the eye. And best of all, you know the Maker, the Master of the Universe. He holds the future, and He holds the answers. We merely wait on Him. End-time patience.

When the Holy Spirit begins to bring His fruit into your life, this end-time patience is one of the first things to appear. That is true because end-time patience begins to blossom at the moment you finally realize that God is eternal and that He offers eternity to you. That moment changes your perspective once and for all. Eternity far surpasses the here and now. And an eternal focus brings end-time patience. Because you know God, you have something worth waiting for.

Social Patience

The second dimension of patience that the Holy Spirit begins to work in each believer's heart is social patience. That means patience with other people—patience with the very real people in your life, right here and right now.

Discover how social patience blossoms directly out of end-time patience. As you learn to have a Kingdom view of the world and of your life, the Spirit then is able to move you to a deeper level of patience with other people. In other words, the more you know God and trust in His eternal ways, the more you are able to be patient with the other people around you. You know the big stuff, so the small stuff begins to occupy your mind a little less. Better yet, you realize that you are still growing in the Lord and others are too. Best of all, you know who holds the future.

The apostle Paul shows how God expects and desires this kind of patience in you: *"As God's chosen ones, holy and beloved,* **clothe yourselves with** *compassion, kindness, humility, meekness,* **and patience. Bear with one another,** *and if anyone has a complaint against another, forgive each other; just as the Lord has forgiven you, so you also must forgive."* (Col. 3:12–13 [NRSV])

Patience originates in the Holy Spirit Himself. And you begin to live in the Holy Spirit at the moment you are baptized. In the first-century Church, men and women stripped naked as they entered the baptismal pool, symbolizing how they were taking off the old self. When they emerged from the baptism, they clothed themselves in a white robe, symbolizing the new self in Christ. That's why Saint Paul here uses the phrase *"clothe yourselves."* When you are becoming the-best-version-of-yourself®, you clothe yourself in patience. That is possible only because of your baptism, when you put on Christ.

And patience means learning to be patient with other people, even to the point of forgiveness. Notice how Saint Paul adds, *"Clothe yourselves with . . . patience. Bear with one another."* In other words, just as God is patient with you and your failures, so too does God desire that you will be patient with your difficult neighbor, your rebellious child, or your opinionated coworker in your struggles to live and be together. Bearing with one another even when shortcomings and failures are apparent—*that* is social patience.

The words of Scripture usually link the three ideas of patience, bearing with one another, and forgiveness. For example, just as he does in Colossians, the apostle Paul in Ephesians 4:1–2 says, *"I . . . urge you to live in a manner worthy of the call you have received, with all humility and gentleness, **with patience, bearing with one another through love**.*" So it seems natural, then, to take a look at how the Spirit will bring out patience and forgiveness in you as you walk in the Spirit.

Peter is a good place to start. Think of Jesus's relationship with the man who would become Saint Peter. In this one relationship alone, Jesus demonstrates how the three concepts of patience, bearing with one another in love, and forgiveness are all linked together.

1) Jesus calls Peter to leave his fishing business and "follow" Him to become a fisher of men. Peter obeys Jesus immediately. (Mark 1:16–20)

2) Peter is a witness as his own mother-in-law is healed by Jesus. (Mark 1:29–31)

3) Peter witnesses firsthand the remarkable life of Jesus as Jesus heals the sick, feeds the multitudes, teaches the crowds, and rebukes the Pharisees. Jesus routinely invests significant amounts of time and energy in Peter.

4) Peter confesses that Jesus is the Messiah when Jesus asks, *"Who do you say that I am?"* Peter clearly has been paying attention and knows Jesus well. Peter knows who Jesus is. (Mark 8:27–30)

5) In spite of the fact that Peter knows who Jesus is, Peter rebukes Jesus for teaching the disciples that the Son of Man must die and rise again. Hear that: Peter rebukes Jesus. Maybe Peter doesn't get it as much as we thought he did. In turn, Jesus rebukes Peter with the famous words, *"Get*

behind me, Satan. You are not thinking as God does, but as human beings do." (Mark 8:31–33)

6) Peter then witnesses Jesus's transfiguration on the mountain when Elijah and Moses appear. He even suggests that booths be built so that everyone can stay on top of that mountain rather than returning to their mundane lives. (Mark 9:2–8)

7) Peter is present when Jesus enters Jerusalem, cleanses the temple, and instructs His followers about the coming crucifixion and end-time. Peter shares in the Lord's Supper in the upper room, when Jesus eats with his disciples for the last time. (Mark 14:12–25)

8) Jesus tells Peter that he will be the one disciple to deny Him. Peter rejects that word and even says that he is willing to go to death with Jesus. Knowing full well that Peter will fail, Jesus is nevertheless patient with Peter's braggadocio. (Mark 14:27–31)

9) Jesus is patient with him even as Peter falls asleep in the Garden of Gethsemane while Jesus prepares to die. In spite of simple instructions to stay awake, Peter has to be awakened by Jesus three separate times. (Mark 14:32–42)

10) As the end nears, Peter denies Jesus not once but three times. (Mark 14:66–72)

11) Finally, Peter is nowhere to be found as Jesus is crucified, dies, and is buried. (Mark 15:33–16:8)

What is the point of all this? Very simple: Peter ebbs and flows. He shows signs of greatness as he leads the disciples. He shows remarkable weakness as he fails Jesus and even denies Him. Peter shows great insight by knowing and understanding who Jesus is. Yet he shows a huge gap in understanding by telling Jesus that the Son of Man should not suffer and die. Remarkably, Jesus stands by Peter. He does not give up on Peter or cast him out of the followers. Jesus is patient as Peter ebbs and flows. Jesus is constant;

He is patient. Always. Even to the end. Because God is patient.

Even when Jesus knows that Peter will deny Him, still He takes Peter along to the Garden of Gethsemane. Still He is patient with Peter, even to the end. And when Peter is broken down and seemingly lost after denying Jesus three times, the risen Jesus returns to make a special appearance to him. Their conversation goes something like this:

> Jesus: "Simon, son of John, do you love me more than these?"
> Peter: "Yes, Lord, you know that I love you."
> Jesus: "Feed my lambs."

> Jesus: "Simon, son of John, do you love me?"
> Peter: "Yes, Lord, you know that I love you."
> Jesus: "Tend my sheep."

> Jesus: "Simon, son of John, do you love me more than these?"
> Peter: "Yes, Lord, you know everything. You know that I love you."
> Jesus: "Feed my sheep." (John 21.15ff)

To the very end, Jesus is patient with Peter. Most stunningly of all, Jesus restores him to the leadership role among the followers. Jesus is patient time and again with Peter. Even when Peter has seemingly dropped the ball in the worst way, Jesus still has the last word. And that word is redemption. Patience.

When Peter falters or stumbles, still Jesus is there. When Peter rebukes or denies Jesus, still Jesus bears with Him in love. And in the end, Jesus forgives Peter. Patience, bearing with one another in love, and forgiveness, the three components of social patience. Patience with others. God shows us what that looks like in Jesus. And God desires to grow that same kind of patience in each of you. Amazing, isn't it?

In the same way that Jesus stood by Peter and loved him even in the face of denial and failure, the Spirit of God brings forth fruit in you even when you fail God. Even as you learn to bear with other people in difficult circumstances. Even as you learn to forgive someone when you don't want to do so. This is a hard lesson. It is true nevertheless. God wants to grow His patience in you. His Spirit will do just that. God is patient. Always.

Being patient with those who hurt you, with the boss who overlooks you, with the parent who does not recognize your achievement and love, and with the neighbor who shuns you are not natural human things to do. Bearing with people who mistreat you and showing patience with difficult people are not natural human responses. They are the work of the Spirit alone. You cannot do these things without the Spirit of God in your life. However, with the Spirit, you cannot help but grow more patient and forgiving with all of these people in your life. It will happen. Why? Because God is patient. The very same remarkable patience that God showed with Peter, He will share with you.

If you are growing in the Spirit, then you will be growing in forgiveness and in bearing with others in love. There is no way around it. If your life is cooperating with the Holy Spirit, you will grow in patience. Remember, the Spirit grows all of His fruit in the heart of each believer. Patience will be part of your blessing from God. You may not be perfect at patience. But you will be growing in it. It is not optional; God does it! It is not of your own power; it is a gift of God's grace.

You will be more patient and forgiving of the failures and shortcomings of others this year than you were last year. And next year you will show more signs of growth in your forgiveness and social patience than you have this year. And the year after that will be more fruitful than the year before it. That is the work of the Spirit. That is social patience.

Personal Endurance and Patience

Now for the toughest part of patience, but also the most rewarding part.

The work of the Spirit brings a patience that goes even deeper than the end-time patience that tells us God wins in the end. And the work of the Spirit brings a patience larger even than the patience we have with the other people in our lives. The work of the Spirit bears fruit as we learn to be patient and endure through personal suffering.

The Spirit makes Himself known to us as we learn to experience the hand of God in our suffering rather than *in spite* of our suffering. This lesson may be the hardest one to hear and the hardest to learn, but it is also the most fruitful. God can and does grow your patience by using the suffering in your life to draw you closer to Him and to form you in His image. God does not *cause* you suffering, but He can *use* it to grow you.

Achieving this level of fruit is a sign of maturity in your life as a Christian. When you can endure personal suffering and still look God in the eye with a heart full of thanksgiving and joy, that is personal endurance and patience generated only by the Holy Spirit. When you can look at the agonizing death of Jesus on Calvary's cross and see God's suffering salvation, that is a life-changing experience. It is a remarkable thing to live in the knowledge that God can and does work for His good in all things. Again, the letters of Paul provide great wisdom. Hear these simple words. Then say them aloud.

Rejoice always.

Pray without ceasing.

*In all circumstances give thanks for this is the will of God for
you in Christ Jesus.*

(1 Thess. 5:16–18)

The hardest part of this personal patience is the fact that it
almost always comes through suffering. I do not know why. I
do not invite it. I certainly do not encourage it in my own life.
I rarely meet anyone who asks God to send more suffering. Yet
somehow through the Holy Spirit, time and again, the hand of
God uses the worst times in my own life to grow my spirit and
to bring about more fruit, especially patience. The deepest lessons often have come through the University of Life and Hard
Knocks. Some things simply cannot be learned in a book. Some
things you will learn only when you live them.

God is good. I not only know that to be true; I know that to
be true in all things. And I learned that to be the case in the worst
three years of my life. Anita, my wife, and I have lived fairly easy
lives, to be honest. However, for three years we endured intense
personal suffering in a way we hope never to replicate. At the
same time, that period of suffering has served over time to grow
our faith lives more than anything either of us has ever experienced. Through that suffering, we learned patience, we deep-
ened our love for each other, and we learned about the heart of a
God who walks alongside us in the valley of the shadow of death.
In short, she and I gained an entirely new way of looking at the
cross of Jesus.

For three years, while I was in graduate school in New Haven,
Connecticut, we lived more than a thousand miles away from our
families at a time when our two daughters were in their infant
and preschool years. We expected that distance to bring some
challenges, but we never expected to learn the faith lessons that

we did.

During those years, my body was afflicted with an intense, chronic case of ulcerative colitis. A case that we and our doctors were never able to get under control, not even with experimental treatments and megadoses of steroids. A case that caused me to spend several hours each day in the bathroom writhing in pain and bleeding, as I watched my body shed thirty pounds. It began to affect the lives and outlook of our young daughters and ultimately resulted in my having my entire colon removed and replaced by a bag that I will wear on my body each day for the rest of my life as a simple reminder of the battle.

At the same time, during these three years, Anita suffered two miscarriages. In fact, there was one day when both of us lay in the same hospital, doors apart, undergoing medical procedures while a caring relative took care of our girls. We had never felt so helpless.

Things only got worse a few months later, when another doctor diagnosed me with an early case of melanoma, the skin cancer that kills. Fortunately, that diagnosis came early enough that the treatments could provide a cure.

It is hard to describe, hard to imagine, really, but somehow, through this period of being isolated from family while enduring a crucible of physical suffering, we each experienced the hand of God in a new and vital way. To some, that statement will make no sense. Others will nod in quick agreement.

Through the love and assurance of friends in our new town, through the prayers of other believers scattered around the globe, and through the presence of the Holy Spirit in our darkest hours, somehow I grew closer to God. Even more remarkably, God worked to rearrange my priorities and help me to see what is truly of value in this lifetime. A number of things that I had previously hoped to do in my life and my ministry suddenly fell by the wayside, for I realized that God had clearly given me the mission of sharing the Gospel of Good News about Jesus and that many of the other things in my life were a distraction.

Since I no longer knew for sure how long I might live, God made it quite clear to me that it was time to get on with the task He had given me. In the face of death, I learned a healthy impatience for the things of life that simply do not matter. More important, I learned to be patient when things looked dark or bleak. God is still in control, and I can trust Him. In other words, I learned a deep, abiding patience. Because I had nowhere else to go but to God.

Doctors could not help; my education could not help; my ambitions and goals could not help. Only God could be my help and my hope. He taught me that patience. Without suffering, I would never have learned that.

It is true for me, and it is true for you, just as it was true for the apostle Paul. How else to explain these verses written by Saint Paul from prison?

> But whatever gains I had, these I have come to consider a loss because of Christ. More than that, **I even consider everything as a loss because of the supreme good of knowing Christ Jesus my Lord.** For his sake I have accepted the loss of all things, and I consider them so much rubbish, that I may gain Christ. (Phil. 3:7–8)

> . . . to know him and the power of his resurrection and the **sharing of his sufferings by being conformed to his death.** (Phil. 3:10)

How else would Paul have the ability to demonstrate patience and peace with great personal suffering other than by the work of the Holy Spirit? Remember, Paul is in prison as he writes this. He is unable to fulfill the mission that God has given him, and he is withering alone in a prison cell. Yet, somehow, Paul is prospering in Christ.

He is filled with the joy of knowing Jesus better through His suffering for the Gospel's sake. I know no one on earth who could exhibit such patience in these circumstances by any means other than the Holy Spirit. And the Spirit was able to produce this personal patience and endurance in Paul's soul through tremendous sufferings that go far beyond imprisonment. Beatings, lashings, shipwrecks, and stonings—Paul endured them all and did so with a patience borne only by the Holy Spirit out of suffering.

In 2 Corinthians, Paul reminds the Corinthians of his afflictions, hardships, calamities, floggings, lashings, beatings, stonings, shipwrecks, robberies, and starvations on behalf of the Church and his personal mission for Jesus. Yet Paul comes out of these events loving God more and desiring Jesus more fully. Paul endures the worst of life and emerges even more passionate about his mission. Now, that is Spirit work.

It will be true for you too. When you walk in the Spirit, the Spirit turns the worst parts of your life into opportunities for bearing fruit to become the-best-version-of-yourself®. More often than not, that fruit is patience. You will learn to trust God in all things, and to live by Him and through Him rather than on your own timetable and according to your own plans. God is patient, and He desires to grow that patience in your life and soul.

And it is that patience that allows the believer not only to hear but truly to understand and believe that indeed *"all things work for good for those who love God, who are called according to his purpose."* (Rom. 8:28) Indeed, all things do work together for good, because God is good. As your patience grows, that simple fact of God's goodness grows. That is the work of the Spirit, the Holy Spirit of God, the Spirit who brings personal endurance and patience.

The Holy Spirit did that same work in the prophets who endured suffering to speak truth in the name of the Lord. There is no better example of the blessings that come from endurance than Jeremiah. He endured and was faithful even in the face of complete failure and rejection by the world.

Faithfulness to God can bring no results. We do not like to hear that, but it is true. Jeremiah worked for years to speak God's truth. When Judah faced destruction by the Babylonians, Jeremiah preached the message of repentance, calling the Jews to fall down on their knees before God. Judah failed to listen to Jeremiah. Jeremiah stayed true to the message God gave him, and yet the people of Judah refused to listen and eventually rejected Jeremiah completely.

We like results. We like to see the fruits of our labors. No one likes to work hard and see nothing come from that work. Yet sometimes our hardest work for God yields nothing. We stand up for truth, we work hard, and still the powers of evil seem to prevail. Nevertheless, God still calls us to be faithful. That's personal patience and endurance.

Faithfulness to God can bring hostility. The more Jeremiah preached, the more hostility he endured. Yet he remained faithful—so faithful that he continued to preach throughout his life even in the face of greater and more violent opposition. He endured imprisonment, exile, and death threats. He endured attacks. And still he remained faithful to God's word and truth.

We do not like to be attacked. We go out of our way to avoid conflict. We prefer the comfort of popularity and choose the path of least resistance. Yet, the call of God can and does lead to resistance, rejection, even attack. It is that kind of personal endurance and patience that God seeks to work in you and in me. In fact, it seems clear that the closer you get to the heart of God, the more the world will attack you. And the more you are attacked, the closer still God draws you to Him. And in that drawing near, God shapes you to be more patient, trusting in Him alone for the future and for the victory. You can be patient for your stand with God.

In the end, the Spirit draws us close to God. That is how we become the-best-version-of-ourselves. The farther you walk with God, the more you learn to stay the course and trust Him to provide. The more you grow in the Spirit, the more patience you have, for you slowly grow to understand that God really is in control.

We do not know everything now, but we shall know later. Trust in God; allow end-time patience to saturate your life. Let God lead you to greater levels of personal endurance and patience. That is God's heart. God is patient. And God will grow patience in you. And you will become the-best-version-of-yourself®.

GROWING A LIFE OF PATIENCE

1. **Cultivate and memorize simple prayers to use during stressful times.** When life is crazy around you, the kids are screaming, the phone is ringing, the traffic is not moving, the enemies are attacking, call those simple prayers to mind and allow God's Spirit to saturate your life. Memorize prayers like: "Come, Lord Jesus, come" or *"I love you, Lord"* or *"We know that all things work for good for those who love God, who are called according to his purpose."* (Romans 8:28)

2. **Take in slow, deep breaths as a bodily way to inhale the Spirit of God.** When stress builds and impatience grows, remind yourself of the patient presence of God by using slow, deep breaths to fill your body and enlarge your heart and soul. Breathe in

the Spirit of God and allow it to permeate your body and soul. Feel the Spirit move through you, bringing hope and new life. Patience will grow.

3. **Don't sweat the small stuff.** I heard that basic message years ago from a wise pastor. Now it is a best-selling book. However, we can never learn to let go of the small stuff that overtakes us without God in our lives. Better yet, as my boyhood pastor taught me, "It's all small stuff." End-time patience teaches us that God holds the details of the world in His hands and is at work for a much larger purpose. Everything else is just details. Remind yourself to let it go.

4. **Embrace failure.** Stumbling and falling can help you grow personally and even learn to accept the failures of others. I hate to fail; you hate to fail. None of us likes others to see us fail or fall short. However, if we are growing and stretching for God, we will fail. We may even fail often. If we are not failing at something, we are not trying. Accept that and use it to grow. When you come to terms with your own failures and shortcomings, you will soon find yourself being more patient with other people around you who fall short. Accept your own imperfections, learn to accept those of others, and soon patience will blossom in your own life.

5. **Make a forgiveness list.** Pray daily for those who have hurt you or let you down. This will grow your patience more than anything else you can do. Pray first for those for whom it is easiest to pray. Over time, God will shape your heart to allow you to pray for those who have wounded you and hurt you the most deeply. As you continue to pray, God's Spirit will move in you to grow patience with others.

KINDNESS

"... the fruit of the Spirit is love, joy, peace, patience, KINDNESS, generosity, faithfulness, gentleness, self-control ..." Galatians 5:22–23

Kindness

5. EASY TO BE HARD

Why does something that sounds so easy always seem so hard?

"Love your neighbor as yourself." Why does something that sounds so easy always seem so hard? The world abounds with evidence that we find it tough to love other people at all. Divorces. Assaults. Bullies. Wars. Lawsuits. Kindness seems to be in short supply.

At its worst, the world is nasty, violent, and harsh. Teachers now have to be trained to protect themselves against attacks from their students. Fathers assault referees at youth ball games. Blogs bristle with vitriol and insults. Overflowing prisons burst at the seams because we cannot control the mayhem in our streets. Grotesque violence fills the images on our movie screens and television sets. A visitor to earth could easily make the case that unkindness defines the planet.

However, unkindness is not just "out there" in the world. More often than not, unkindness shows itself in very simple, everyday ways. We make rude hand gestures and mutter obscenities at one another while we wait in traffic. We hurry to nose our cart in to be next in line at the grocery store. We gossip about our coworkers at the coffee machine.

Why do we treat other people as if they don't matter? The

answer is shockingly simple: We love ourselves more than we love anyone else. We are still not quite sure that other people matter as much as we do. That is the sin of pride: loving ourselves most of all. C. S. Lewis called pride "the complete anti-God state of mind." When you focus on yourself, it can be very difficult to notice God or the people around you.

Ironically, in times of war, the veil of unkindness often peels away and is replaced by unity. When our nation goes through a crisis, like the Islamic terror attacks of September 11, 2001, we stop and refocus our hearts and attention on things that "really matter." People slow down, offer consoling words, assist a person in need. Suddenly, we notice the people around us and realize that life is short. For a moment, as if it were Christmas Day, being kind to one another becomes the order of the day. Isn't that odd? In good times, we find it difficult to be kind. In times of war, kindness becomes commonplace, as if there's some cosmic seesaw of kindness and violence that has to balance out.

Why is that? It is very simple: When we focus on the things that really matter, we realize that human beings, human life, the people around us are what really matter. All the other things that used to seem so pressing become less important, and we take stock for a moment of the other people in our lives. Then we show kindness. In other words, when we really value life and seek to love other people, kindness becomes a priority. When we are kind we show that we value other people as much as we value ourselves. They are just as important as we are. Kindness flows out of recognizing the simple truth that people—all kinds of people—matter. We were all made by the same God and made in His image.

We all matter to God. Once you realize that, kindness comes easily.

What Kindness Is: Ephesians 2:7

God is kind.

Ephesians 2:7 reveals that God shows us *"the immeasurable riches of his grace in* **kindness** *to us in Christ Jesus."* God is kind, and Jesus is the living proof of that kindness. Jesus displays what God's kindness looks like. Jesus presents God's kindness in living form. Even though we may be unkind to other people, or even to God Himself, God still takes the first step and gives us the unmistakably kind gift of Jesus.

There are four key parts to this important biblical statement:

1) Immeasurable riches

When God saw the world struggling, wandering off on its own, lost in traps of its own making, He sent Jesus to show the way home. God offered Jesus to the world then, and He offers Jesus to you and me now. When you are lost, God sends Jesus to find you. When you turn your back on God, still He calls you home with the kind gift of Jesus: God's own son, the Word of God made flesh, offered as a gift to the world. That is only the beginning of the "immeasurable riches" God bestows on us.

In fact, in Ephesians 1:3ff, Saint Paul shares the details of these immeasurable riches: God has blessed us in Christ with every spiritual blessing in the heavenly places; He chose us in Christ before the foundation of the world; He destined us for adoption as His children through Jesus Christ; we have redemption through His blood; we receive forgiveness of our trespasses; He lavishes His grace upon us; He has made known to us the mystery of His will; in Christ, we have obtained an inheritance; and we have been marked with the seal of the Holy Spirit.

Jesus is grace beyond compare: a God who offersh His son not merely to the entire world, but even to you. That is divine kindness, kindness even when you turn away or are unkind to God.

Who can possibly put a value on that? By definition, Christians are "immeasurably rich."

2) Kindness

Webster's focuses its definition of *kind* around the quality of being good-hearted. Kindness and love are first cousins, alongside goodness and gentleness. But kindness is more of a state than an act. Kindness, or having a good heart, lives itself out in loving, good, gentle ways and acts. Very simply, kindness is a "heart condition" more than anything else.

We know God's heart. We have seen His heart in Jesus. Because God is kind, He shows us His heart in the goodness, love, and gentleness of Jesus.

3) Toward us

God values you. He values each life He creates. And His heart's desire is that we will value one another too. Indeed, God's kindness toward you is meant to lead you to repentance (Rom. 2:4). God's kindness intends and expects a response.

Remember, again, Jesus's greatest commandment: *"Love God . . . AND love your neighbor as yourself."* Love God. Love people. Love other people as much as you love you. Jesus's message has kindness at its core: *"See other lives as just as important as your own and treat them accordingly."*

Jesus shared that supreme divine kindness with each person He met. Think about the people with whom Jesus spent most of His time: children, lepers, sick women, men possessed by demons, tax collectors, prostitutes, and sinners. Hardly a list of the rich, famous, and powerful. No, Jesus spent the bulk of His time with a ragtag, motley crew of oddballs and misfits. But lest we think that Jesus failed to notice the powerful or popular, He also welcomed the wealthy and the important, but on His own terms rather than theirs. Jesus shows us the kind heart of God as He welcomes the smallest and largest alike, as He loves even the most sinful.

His message was so very simple, but it is still hard for humans to comprehend: Every single human being, every life created by God matters to God. No one is more important or significant or valued than any other. Here's the catch: If each person matters to God, each human should matter to us. *That* God-centered "heart condition," in which you see the image of God in each person, alone produces kindness.

4) In Christ Jesus

If Jesus is God's kindness, then God's big gift of kindness came in a small package of swaddling clothes, a baby sent to save us. God is so kind that Jesus did not count equality with God as something to be grasped and therefore emptied Himself of His place in heaven. Jesus became flesh (John 1:14). His very enfleshment personified kindness.

Jesus represents the kindness of a God who became one of us. Religions have famous teachers and prophets. Religions have teachings about God. But only the Christian faith professes that God became flesh as the supreme act of kindness toward His creatures. He came to us so that we could come to Him. God's loving gift of Jesus to you is a miraculous act of kindness that sets the tone for your life.

In fact, that is what Jesus does. He shows you God. In order to help you become the-best-version-of-yourself, Jesus will guide you home. He will embody in Himself who and what you are called to be. He is the Word of God made flesh, living right here among us.

The fact that God decided to become like you demonstrates

that He values human beings. He did not come as some kind of alien or foreign being. He came first as a fetus in Mary's womb, then as a baby born in a manger, then as a child, and then as a man. God became fully one of us. That means He values humans. And God values you. Jesus is God's supreme gift of kindness to you. Jesus embodies the very kindness of God. He is God's living kindness.

God sent Jesus to seek and to save you. Like the woman looking for a coin she has lost, or the shepherd looking for *one* sheep who has strayed from the flock, so too does a kind God look high and low for you (Luke 15). God desires you, seeks you, loves you, even when you turn away. Remember that kindness is a state of being, and God's kindness shapes His actions: He sends Jesus to bring you home.

The seeking presence of Jesus is God's supreme act of kindness. That is what Jesus does. He expresses God's kindness toward you by searching for you, claiming you, and showing you the ways of God. That is what we were made for: to live with Jesus in the ways of God.

In the end, God's kindness is intended to change you. *"Or do you hold his priceless kindness, forbearance, and patience in low esteem, unaware that the kindness of God would lead you to repentance?"* (Rom. 2:4)

1) God is kind to you because He loves you.

2) God is kind to you because He hopes that you will turn from your unkindnesses toward Him. God yearns for you to love Him as He loves you. God is kind to you even when you are unkind to Him.

3) God is kind to you because He hopes that His kindness will change you. And that change begins the journey toward becoming the-best-version-of-yourself. That is why He is kind.

When you stray, God is still there, kindly offering Jesus to you. That is divine kindness. Kindness is Jesus.

What Kindness Is Not: 1 Peter 2:1–3

Ephesians teaches you the divine kindness of God. Jesus is God's living kindness. In 1 Peter, you discover what human kindness looks like by seeing what kindness is not: *"Rid yourselves of all malice and all guile, insincerity, envy, and all slander; like newborn infants, long for pure spiritual milk, so that through it you may grow into salvation;* **for you have tasted the kindness of the Lord.***"* (1 Pt. 2:1–3: translation my own)

You taste the fruit of God's kindness when you embrace and love Jesus. He touches your heart with the kindness of God, a God who loves you before you even know who He is. A God who loves and desires you even when you are remarkably unkind yourself. Jesus touches you and makes you whole. His kindness overwhelms, unlike anything else in this world. Jesus is kind because God is kind. And God wants that same kindness to take root in your life and mine.

What does that kindness look like? Peter makes it plain.

When you become the-best-version-of-yourself, you will:

1) Rid yourself of malice.

Malice means intent to injure. God does not seek to injure people. God's Spirit does not seek ways to harm others. God's people will put away the desire to hurt others and instead begin to grow in kindness. Where others make fun of the last child picked to be on a team, kindness will offer encouragement and grace. Your kindness will seek to help, not hurt.

It's true on the playground; it's even true in divorce. Have you seen the bumper sticker that reads, "I still miss my ex-wife, but my aim is improving"? Evidently, the sticker's creator still has a little malice that needs to be put away.

The fruit of the Spirit is kindness. Kindness is encouraging, building up, aiding. God's kindness intends to build up others, not hurt them.

2) Rid yourself of guile.

Guile is deceitfulness. God does not deceive. God is open, transparent, and straightforward. However, humans often deal in deception. You deceive when you negotiate unscrupulously in business. You deceive when you do not reveal your behaviors and misdeeds to your spouse. You deceive when you fail to tell the whole truth. While the world will say, "Caveat emptor: Let the buyer beware," the-best-version-of-yourself will embrace the kindness to deal openly and truthfully.

When my wife and I bought our first house, we were quickly initiated into the mysteries of real estate: commissions, inspections, termites, flood plains, and surveys. We learned a lot about disclosures too.

On the disclosure sheet, the seller of the house comments on each area of the house (e.g., foundation, roof, plumbing) he or she is selling. The seller is supposed to disclose any past problems or current issues affecting any part of the house. In our case, the seller made comments in each area but left blank the section regarding the home's roof. We soon learned in our inspection that the roof had numerous leaks causing lots of damage, which the seller said he simply "forgot" to disclose. That is deception by omission, guile.

The fruit of the Spirit is kindness. Kindness is being straightforward and truthful. God's kindness is upright and true. His people will be too.

3) Rid yourself of insincerity.

Insincerity is dishonesty, or lack of genuineness. You are insincere when you give false praise or when you fail to tell things accurately. You are insincere when you make others believe things about you that simply are not true or are embellishments of who you really are. Insincerity arrives when you pretend to like someone whom you deeply resent and distrust. While the world offers false praise and flattery to someone important in hopes of personal gain and recognition, kindness remains humbly quiet, resting on the values of God rather than the values of the world.

The fruit of the Spirit is kindness. Kindness is being genuine and true. God's kindness is sincere. His people will be too.

4) Rid yourself of envy.

Envy is the selfish resentment of what another person enjoys. Envy begrudges others who have more than you do or are more fortunate than you are. Envy bears grudges against those who win when you do not. Envy secretly hates those who are good at the things you are not good at. Envy eats at the heart from the inside out. Envy corrodes and destroys.

Jeff and Bob had similar dreams. Both wanted to go to the same prestigious law school. When Bob was admitted but Jeff was not, Jeff's heart ached so badly that he ended the friendship and moved away. He could not bear his own disappointment, nor could he celebrate Bob's success. His envy simply overwhelmed him, and he dragged that burden behind him for years.

While the world begrudges, kindness rejoices in the successes and achievements of others. While the world resents the beautiful new home of a brother, kindness offers to celebrate a housewarming to share in the joy. Clearly, kindness is not man-made; it is possible only through God's heart-changing Spirit.

The fruit of the Spirit is kindness. Kindness rejoices in the good fortune and success of others. God's kindness celebrates gladly.

5) Rid yourself of slander.

Slander injures someone by false report. When I try to make myself look good by making others look bad, that is slander. Slander disregards the truth and desires to hurt. Slander willingly and gladly destroys another person's good character and good name. Ironically, slander also destroys the character and good name of the slanderer. And sadly, slander has become a cottage industry in the American world of celebrities and blogospheres.

While the world drags the name of enemies through the mud and the media, kindness looks for the high road, even remaining silent in the face of slander rather than injuring another for no cause. While the world spreads misinformation about rivals or competitors, kindness seeks to compete in an open and fair way.

The fruit of the Spirit is kindness. Kindness praises and commends. God's kindness looks for the good and praises it.

You have tasted the kindness of the Lord. That is a remarkable thing. God has forgiven you when you were dishonest. God has overlooked your envy of others. God has not held your insincere tongue against you. Instead of crushing you, God has been kind to you. God has given you Jesus. And with Jesus comes change— a change of heart, a change of ways, a change of life. Experience life in God's kindness and discover that you are on your way to becoming the-best-version-of-yourself.

Jesus brings the kindness of God into your heart. As that kindness takes root in your life, it will flow from your heart. It can be no other way; kindness is a fruit of God's Spirit. A consistently unkind person does not live in Jesus or walk in the Spirit of God. How do you know? Because God is kind. And His children are too.

Kindness Lived Out in Word and Action: Joshua 2

When Moses died, Joshua took over the reins of leadership for Israel. He was understandably nervous. He had never led before. Moses had always been in charge. And now they were about to enter the promised land. What a burden of responsibility Joshua faced.

The Israelites were nervous too. They were at the most important point in their history, and now they had a new leader. With Moses, they had known what to expect. But now Joshua was at the helm, and it was time to cross the Jordan River into the land of Canaan. All God's promises were coming to pass, but first they had to trust Joshua to take them there.

Joshua was scared. The Israelites were scared. And the promised land lay just ahead.

What was the first thing Joshua did? He prayed.

What was the second? He appointed two spies to secretly enter the city of Jericho to see what lay ahead. The spies spent the night at the house of a prostitute named Rahab.

When the King of Jericho got word of two foreign spies in his city, he sent word to Rahab to turn the Israelite spies over to him. However, Rahab knew that these spies were on God's side, that they were agents for the work of God in the world and in her life. She understood she had a simple choice: to stand with God or against Him. She chose to stand with God. Rahab chose to be a part of what God was doing even if it cost her enormously.

So she protected the men from the king's soldiers, hid the spies in her home, helped them to escape from Jericho safely, and then prevented the king from finding out about the Israelites' plan. She risked her own life, extended hospitality to the two Israelites, and stood firmly with God. Why? She said, *"The Lord your God is God in heaven above and on earth below."* (Josh. 2:11) Rahab knew exactly what she was doing. She was turning from her ugly past to a bright new future with God.

Rahab showed kindness to God by showing kindness to His people. In Joshua 2:12, she specifically mentions that she has dealt "kindly" with the Israelites and hopes that they in turn will deal "kindly" with her. Indeed, they do. When Jericho is taken over by the people of Israel, Rahab and her family are made a part of the people of God (Josh. 6:5). Rahab is welcomed as a part of God's people. In other words, she finds her way home.

Rahab's kindness reflects the kindness of God. She is held in such esteem that she ultimately is even listed as an ancestor of Jesus in Matthew 1:5. A foreign Canaanite woman, earning her living as a prostitute, sides with God, acts in kindness, and becomes a part of God's own people. Then Jesus is borne from her line. A remarkable story. Kindness.

What does this story of Rahab teach us about kindness?

First, kindness is active, not passive. To move toward becoming the-best-version-of-yourself, you will engage life, not sit idly by and hope for change. God is not a passive, do-nothing God. The Holy Spirit changes you, and those changes will make you behave differently. Faith is no spectator sport. Kindness acts; it takes the initiative.

Second, kindness takes risks for God, even in the face of hostility or danger. Kindness recognizes God's work and seeks to be a part of that. Kindness hospitably takes God's people in, and protects them from that which would harm them. In other words, kindness often swims upstream against the world. Rahab was willing to be kind to God's people because she hoped that God would in turn be kind to her. She recognized the work of God and chose to become a part of it, even when she had to put her own life on the line. Kindness is courageous.

In the same way, becoming the-best-version-of-yourself will

require courage and risk. A ship is safe as long as it sits in the harbor, but that's not what ships are made for. Your life will be comfortable as long as you remain where you are. Change and growth take courage.

The world is often harsh and violent, so it takes courage to be kind. Where the world might criticize a Christian as being a doormat, softy, or pushover, a Christian knows that kindness requires signifcant strength and great courage. Kindness often requires the greatest strength of all: to stand with God in the face of criticism or persecution. Kindness comes from the heart of God.

However, the New Testament makes kindness even more clear. You do not have to earn God's kindness like Rahab tried to do. Instead, God is already kind toward you. Remember? God offers Jesus Christ to you. Your kindness to other people merely reflects the kindness that God has already shown you in Jesus. Your kindness is genuine and true because you love and serve a God who has been eternally kind to you. Thus, you can face hostility, even violence, and return it with kindness, because your trust and hope are in a God whose ways are kind. You stand with God.

You have tasted the kindness of the Lord. His Holy Spirit frees you to be courageously kind. And the-best-version-of-yourself takes the risk to do just that.

GROWING A LIFE OF KINDNESS

1. Think before you speak. Your grandmother was right: If you cannot say something kind, say nothing at all. That requires thinking before you speak. And it requires thinking before you act, so that you avoid words or deeds that flow from impulse or emotion. Ask yourself: "Will my words harm anyone? Will my actions injure?" Remember how Joshua prayed before doing anything when he took over the reins of leadership from Moses. Kindness seeks to build up rather than injure.

2. Listen, really listen. Spend time with a child. Actually spend time with him. Put away the cell phone and the calendar. Turn off the television or the car radio. Listen. Listen carefully. Listen well. Show kindness by demonstrating to a child that she matters. There is no more valuable gift or expression of kindness than to really listen.

3. Practice "random acts of kindness." They can be remarkably powerful. Pay someone's bill at a restaurant or the toll of the driver behind you on a highway. Pick up the trash in your neighbor's yard. Wash your teenager's car. Share a kind word with the cashier at the grocery store. Assist a mother with children by holding the door open. Look for small ways at various times throughout the day to share a small sample of God's kindness and grace with a complete stranger or a good friend. You will inject a measure of God's kindness and grace into their world. Best of all, you will be surprised at how that kindness finds its way back into your life.

4. Start each day in prayer. Ask God to help you see the world as your place to minister rather than as a place to fear. Like Rahab, you can be an agent of kindness. See the people around you as persons in need of God's kindness rather than as mere things or objects in your life. Listen to the friend whose father has just died; share a meal with the neighbor just diagnosed with cancer; assist the family struggling to stay afloat after a job layoff; notice the children at school who don't get invited or included. In other words, offer kindness to the same people whom Jesus noticed and valued. Then you will be living in the Holy Spirit.

5. Try to live one day with no lies of any kind. Notice how hard it is to be truthful and kind! Notice the remarkable level of attention, energy, and restraint that it takes. We are used to fudging, cutting corners, and offering empty flattery or white lies. Honesty may mean sharing difficult news. Kindness may mean choosing to say nothing at all. God is straightforward and true.

GENEROSITY

". . . the fruit of the Spirit is love, joy, peace, patience, kindness, GENEROSITY, faithfulness, gentleness, self-control . . ." Galatians 5:22–23

Generosity

6. THE HAPPIEST PEOPLE I KNOW

Why did she rise early every day simply to
give the fruits of her labor away?

God is good. All the time.

Generosity created the universe. God is the Author of Life. He formed us from the dust of the earth and breathed into us the breath of life. God looked at His creation and saw that it was *"very good."* (Gen. 1:31) Creation is good because God is generous.

If God is generous, then it just makes sense that generosity would be a fruit of His Spirit. God made you in His image, so you have the ability to be generous. But at the same time, like every human being, you sin, you turn away from God, you serve other gods or yourself, and you often fail to honor God. The Bible describes sin as "missing the mark." God has a dream for your life, but when you fail to love and obey Him, you miss the mark. That is what sin is: Rather than seeking to be good and to do good, we humans often fall short of God's dreams for us. Just as we can become the-best-version-of-ourselves, we also carry the capacity to fail to even try.

Even when we try to do God's will, there frequently is something inside us that leads us astray. Romans 7:15 describes that inner struggle when Paul writes, *"What I do, I do not understand. For I do not do what I want, but I do what I hate."* Generosity is hard, isn't it? We want to be be good, but on our own, we simply cannot achieve the full goodness that is within us.

We fall short of God's dreams, and that is where Jesus comes in. To discuss generosity, Jesus provides the starting point, for He Himself is a gift of God's immeasurable giving.

Merciful Goodness

Jesus teaches us about generosity in three ways.

1) God's Merciful Generosity Toward Us

Like all humans, you are a sinner. You fall short of the glory of God. While you may want to please God and serve Him, somehow you get sidetracked. God invites you to a life full of joy, peace, and love: He calls you to the-best-version-of-yourself. Yet you often find yourself living a life full of anger, greed, and envy instead.

God is holy, and He has a holy dream for your life. Somehow, you take God's beautiful creation of life and twist it, distort it, abuse it, and disregard it. God wants you to have life, but often, because of your sinfulness, it is easy to choose death. By the measure of God's holiness and our sinfulness, we surely deserve to die, for we have all failed God.

So what does God do about it? Does He destroy us? Does He sentence us all to death? No, He makes a new covenant, and covenants are marvelous things. Covenants are better than contracts. Covenants last. Covenants don't break. God makes a new covenant with you in Jesus. And God keeps His promises. Because God is good. All the time.

Remember the words of Romans. The apostle Paul describes God's miraculous and merciful covenant with us, a covenant that God makes because God is good. He shows us that merciful goodness by:

a) allowing Jesus to die in our place for our sins, when it is we who deserve to die; and

b) sending Jesus in spite of the fact that we didn't ask for help, nor did we deserve it.

We were sinners, and God loved us anyway. Jesus is simply a gift of God's merciful goodness—a gift of forgiveness and salvation. God is good, and Jesus proves it: *"But God proves his love for us in that while we were still sinners Christ died for us."* (Rom. 5:8)

And the news gets better. Because God is generous, He not only forgives you for sinfully wasting His creation of life, but He also stands on your side from the moment of your baptism. He takes you in. God makes you His own. He forgives you, restores you, and begins to make you new. He stands with you. Because God is mercifully good. *"If God is for us, who can be against us? He who did not spare his own Son but handed him over for us all, how will he not also give us everything else along with?"* (Rom. 8:31–32)

God's merciful and good covenant cannot be broken. God's love cannot be destroyed or removed from you. It lasts forever, and it supercedes all things. The new covenant is a certain promise of God, because God is good, always. *"For I am convinced that neither death, nor life, nor angels, nor principalities, nor present things, nor future things, nor powers, nor height, nor depth, nor any other creature will be able to separate us from the love of God in Christ Jesus our Lord."* (Rom. 8:38–39)

Think about what God has done. He has made an unbreakable covenant with you. His promise is sure: Receive the gift of Jesus, be forgiven, follow Him, and be made new. You didn't deserve it. You didn't earn it. You didn't even ask for it. God simply gives it. All you do is receive.

That proves God's generosity. Because we are sinners, we deserve to die. Yet God instead gives us new life. God forgives. We deserve wrath, and instead God is merciful. God is good. All the time. In all places. Always.

2) Our Merciful Generosity in Forgiveness

Once you receive God's gift of new life and forgiveness in Jesus, God begins in turn to teach you how to forgive. He begins to make you good just as He is good. He shapes you to help you live up to being made in His own image. And that is when you begin the journey toward becoming the-best-version-of-yourself.

God injects His generosity into you. And His generosity begins with forgiveness. If generosity is the fruit of God's Spirit, then forgiveness is the branch on which generosity grows. A generous heart forgives.

Unfortunately, we humans are not very good at forgiveness. We may, however, be very good at grudge holding. We are often good at holding other people to perfect standards that we cannot possibly meet ourselves. And we excel at letting hurts fester inside us and being perfectionists who criticize anyone at any opportunity.

Humans don't understand mercy very well. We like it when others show mercy and forgiveness to us. But we find it ever so challenging to show mercy and forgiveness to the people around us. Did you hear about the sign in Baltimore located on the wall outside a convent? The sign read: TRESPASSERS WILL BE PROSECUTED TO THE FULLEST EXTENT OF THE LAW— SISTERS OF MERCY. Evidently, even the Sisters of Mercy struggle with mercy.

But God's way is a different way. God forgives. He desires to show you how to forgive also.

Jesus makes it clear: Forgiveness lies at the heart of being a Christian. That makes sense, of course, because forgiveness lies at the very heart of God.

But I say to you that if you are angry with a brother, you will be liable to judgment; and if you insult a brother, you will be liable to the council; and if you say 'You fool' you will be liable to the hell of fire. So when you are offering your gift at the altar, if you remember that your brother has something against you, leave your gift there before the altar and go; **first be reconciled to your brother.** *Then come offer your gift. (Matthew 5:22–24 [NRSV])*

God has shown us the model. *Forgive first.* He did it for you in Jesus. Now He invites you to do the same with your own brothers and sisters. He invites you to be generous with your forgiveness, not to withhold it stingily in some container to be brought out on special occasions—but to liberally distribute it, like water on parched grass. *"Then Peter approaching asked him, 'Lord, if my brother sins against me, how often must I forgive him? As many as seven times?' Jesus answered, "I say to you, not seven times but seventy–seven times.'"* (Matthew 18:21–22)

Unlimited forgiveness! Bountiful mercy! God is good. God abounds in mercy and generosity. His forgiveness proves it. And He desires to give you the same forgiving heart and generous spirit. God desires to make you good. After all, you are made in His image!

3) Our Merciful Generosity in Compassion

God's generosity teaches you to be merciful not only in forgiveness but also in how you see the world. Using God's eyes, see the world with compassion. View the world as a place in need of God's healing mercy and goodness. Notice those who are hurting and those who are broken. God's goodness invites you to be attentive to the least, the last, and the lost. The Holy Spirit provides you with new eyes to see, eyes saturated with generosity and compassion.

Nearly every one of the prophets, from Isaiah and Jeremiah to

Micah and Nahum, spends enormous amounts of energy calling the Israelites to care for orphans and widows, the dying and the weak, and the elderly and the newborn. God's people share God's goodness with all.

Zechariah put it this way: "'Thus says the Lord of hosts: Render true judgment, and show kindness and compassion toward each other. Do not oppress the **widow or the orphan, the alien or the poor;** *do not plot evil against one another in your hearts.' But they refused to listen; they stubbornly turned their backs and stopped their ears so as not to hear." (Zech. 7:9–11a)*

Even when you are not interested, God is still very interested in how you treat those who are forgotten or lost. We may care only about ourselves, but God calls us outside of ourselves to a life of goodness. *Goodness. Mercy. Forgiveness. Generosity. Compassion.* These are God words.

God has taught me this lesson so many times that I have lost count. Like Israel, I am stubborn; I tend not to allow God's Spirit to help me see the world as He sees it. For example, when I attended seminary, my first-year internship placed me as a chaplain at a homeless shelter for families with children. As part of my placement, I spent an evening each week dining and talking with the residents. I listened to the stories of their lives. I heard their hurts and often prayed with families who had lost jobs or homes. Each week, my fellow students and I met with the pastors who led this church. We reflected on what we were learning about God, about life, and about people.

Early in my time there, I shared that I felt outraged that this church would try to help some of these families whom I felt were clearly trying to take advantage of the goodness of the church. Their stories did not add up. They seemed to be angling to get as much from the church as they could, and I thought they should have to prove that they deserved everything they got. The lead pastor of the church very gently and kindly turned to me and said, "I would rather be called a sucker than be called coldhearted."

God calls you to be generous and good, merciful and forgiving, even to those who might take advantage. *Especially* to those who might take advantage. For your generosity may just make the difference in their lives. Withholding your goodness helps no one and may even injure the people God intends for you to help. You do not need to have the "advantage." God alone is sufficient. God is enough. You are not called to be right all the time. You are called to be forgiving and good. Because God is forgiving and good, and He wants to make your heart just like His. *That* is the-best-version-of-yourself.

God's forgiveness is not limited, nor is it parceled out in small doses here and there. His goodness and mercy overflow and abound. He invites you to embrace the same.

Generous Goodness

God's goodness expresses itself in His generosity. God is good, and God is a giver. In fact, He is the Supreme Giver. God spoke the universe into existence. God breathed into you the breath of life. God formed you in your mother's womb. When you were lost, God gave you Jesus to show you the way home. And God prepares all eternity for you. God is a giver. You are made in His image. So the-best-version-of-yourself will be a generous giver too.

All that we have and enjoy in this lifetime has God as its source. When the people of Israel had given abundantly and generously to build God's temple, David prayed and blessed the Lord in the presence of the assembly:

David said, "Blessed are you, O Lord, the God of our ancestor Israel, forever and ever. Yours, O Lord, are the greatness,
the power, the glory, the victory, and the majesty;

for all that is in the heavens and on the earth is yours;

yours is the Kingdom, O Lord, and you are exalted as head
above all.

Riches and honor come from you, and you rule over all.

In your hand are power and might; and it is in your hand to
make great and to give strength to all.

And now, our God, we give thanks to you and praise your
glorious name.

But who am I, and what is my people, that we should be able
to make this freewill offering?

**For all things come from you, and of your own
we have given you."**

(1 Chronicles 29:10–14 [NRSV])

God's goodness expresses itself in everything that we have and
in all the world around us. "All things come from you, O God."
Indeed, God is the Supreme Giver; He is the Source of All. We
belong to Him. He is the Giver of Life. When we grow in God's
goodness, we will grow in giving as well.

The most joyful people also happen to be the most generous.
Generous giving is joy. To give is to become more like God.

God delights in your giving and even multiplies it to bless others. "God loves a cheerful giver. Moreover, God is able to make every grace abundant for you, so that in all things . . . you may have an
abundance for every good work." (2 Cor. 9:7b–8).

Nevertheless, humans like to hoard money, to use resources
on ourselves. We worry about ever having enough and fail to see

that God is the source of all blessings and all things. We like to see our things as "our" things. When you do so you become the ugly, self-absorbed creature who lives in the flesh rather than in God's Spirit. You are not so much physically ugly (although greedy eyes and a stingy face are not very becoming), but just not very enjoyable to be around. Misguided hearts are ugly to behold.

When we are envious—when we want what others have—that just isn't a very pretty trait, is it? When we are envious, we always resent other people; we spend time dwelling on what we don't have. None of us grows up wanting to be stingy or envious, yet we find ourselves living "ugly" lives.

One of my ugly moments arrived when I saw the list of the world's wealthiest two hundred people in high tech. As I read the list, I saw the name of a man I used to work with in business before I left to enter full-time ministry. In fact, we'd started with the same management consulting firm on the exact same day. About the same time that I left to pursue theological studies, he left to start his own software firm. The list showed his net worth to be $220,000,000. Mine? Probably about $14.63!

To be honest, for a moment, I read that list and looked on it with envy. For a few minutes, I allowed myself to recite the if-onlys. "If only I had stayed with the firm . . ." "If only I had accepted that role my friend offered me . . ." "If only I had stayed on the business path . . ." And then I began to reflect on all the "things" I could possess now "if only I had. . . ." Sadly, those moments of reflection revealed a lot about my human soul. Ugly, isn't it?

For a moment, the competitive side of me wanted to earn and get and acquire as much as I could as quickly as I could. My eyes became green with envy. If you asked me what the ugliest human trait is, I would have to say it is greed.

Maybe I find greediness so unappealing because I have

struggled with it so much in my own life. It is a temptation for me to want everything just for me, to hold on to money, to become a scrimping, hoarding, conserving, penurious, stingy, parsimonious miser. To have lots of stuff, to protect and defend it, and to use it only for myself.

And I can tell you where that leads: to a cold heart, a jaundiced eye, a suspicious nature, and a lonely life that can hold very little love. When greed settles in, generosity is forced out. The two cannot coexist. They are unable to be roommates. Jesus said you can serve God or you can serve stuff, but you can't serve both. He was right: We either live in the flesh, or we live in the Spirit. And generosity is a fruit of God's Spirit.

You know what generosity looks like: sharing—gladly, willingly, and with joy. Few of us aspire to be stingy. Nearly all of us hope to be generous. Those hopes come from God. Generosity is part of His dream for you. When you grow in generous giving, you become the-best-version-of-yourself.

Robbie Ray was seventy-seven when I heard about her. Every day for thirteen years Robbie rose at two a.m. to bake her special-recipe cream cheese pound cakes. She baked three to eight cream cheese pound cakes per day. The ingredients cost her four dollars per cake. She baked them, then sold and shipped them to customers all over the country for ten dollars each. She donated one hundred percent of the proceeds to the youth ministry fund at her church.

In thirteen years, Robbie Ray baked over seven thousand cakes and gave more than seventy thousand dollars to touch the lives of students with the love of God. She gave it all away. Then again, it really wasn't hers to begin with, was it? Her goodness overflowed. Her generosity proved it every day.

When asked about her baking, Robbie responded, "My goal is one hundred thousand dollars. After all, baking keeps me going."

Clearly she understood what Winston Churchill meant when he said, "We make a living by what we get; we make a life by what we give." Generous giving indicates goodness. And goodness springs from the Spirit of God. And the Spirit of God spurs you on to become the-best-version-of-yourself.

Why did Robbie Ray do it? Why did she rise early every day simply to give the fruits of her labor away?

It could be for a lot of reasons.

- Do you think it is because we are commanded to give? The Scriptures teach that over and over.

- Do you think it is because Robbie likes to watch God take what she gives and then multiply it to touch the lives of countless others, including children she may never meet on this side of the river? Like Jesus did with the fishes and loaves when He fed the five thousand?

- Do you think it is because she feels called to sacrifice? Maybe Robbie knows there is no such thing as real love or honor without sacrifice.

- Do you think it is because she feels like it is the very least that she can do, given how she has seen others called to give their entire lives for Jesus in mission as priests and religious leaders?

- Do you think it is because she knows that she is a coworker with God, laboring in His vineyard and being a blessing to others? Perhaps she envisions herself standing next to missionaries and Mother Teresa and Pope Benedict XVI as she stands baking in her kitchen each morning.

- Do you think it is because she is a channel of grace and knows that she will therefore be blessed more fully as the grace flows back into her life?

- Do you think it is because Robbie wants to give thanks to God for all that He has done? To express her gratitude to

God for being the Source of All?

- Do you think it is because she wants to overcome the temptation to be idolatrous in her own life? Maybe she knows full well that acquiring stuff just leads to worshipping what we acquire. Our stuff often owns us more than we own it. Robbie may be seeking to overcome that temptation to be consumed by her own stuff.
- Do you think it is because she wants to overcome the temptation to withhold any part of herself from God? Perhaps Robbie understands best of all what it means to be completely given over to God.
- Do you think it is because she wants to grow in the image of God—the God who is first and foremost a giver? A God who gives us life, His son, and even eternity?

It is only my opinion, but I suspect that Robbie Ray saw her baking as a way of abandoning herself fully to God in order to love the Lord with all her heart. She knew that her generosity allowed her to share the goodness of God, that when she was baking and shipping, she was really being the-best-version-of-herself.

God called her to love Him. He had a big dream for her life. And Robbie Ray was doing her best to live a life worthy of that dream.

I see Robbie Ray serving in generosity just like the woman in Mark 14 who came and anointed Jesus with expensive oil, lavishing it on His feet and weeping and caressing them with her hair. All the while, the people around her wondered why she would invest that extravagant oil in Him. She abandoned herself fully and completely to loving the Lord. Her generous giving expressed the goodness growing in her heart.

God is a good and giving God, and generosity is a fruit of God's Spirit. Your generosity expresses that goodness, the goodness of a giving God overflowing in you.

GROWING A LIFE OF GENEROSITY

1. Learn to give generously. Learn to share your financial resources:

A) For God's mission through tithing. If you have never tried tithing (giving ten percent of your income to God's Kingdom), try it for one month. Watch how God uses your measure of goodness in remarkable ways to grow you forward toward the-best-version-of-yourself.

B) To help persons in need around you. Begin to notice the people in need in your life and find ways to help. Do you have a sibling whose family is struggling? Do you have a neighbor who just lost a job? Do you work with a custodian or laborer who can barely provide for his own family? Find the people in your life who are experiencing need, and try to find ways to ease that.

C) By sacrificing some of the abundance you enjoy in your own life in order to advance God's Kingdom in the world. Give up something from your life (an expensive hobby or habit, a valued possession, a regular dining-out experience, etc.) and give the money instead to God as an expression of your love for Him. Abandon yourself to loving God fully, just as Robbie Ray and the woman from Mark 14 did.

2. Have mercy on someone you know whose life has been broken. Help a young unwed mother get training for job skills, or provide support for a woman who is fleeing an abusive husband. Be an instrument of God's mercy and goodness.

3. Stand in unity with Christians who do not enjoy the same abundance, comforts, and freedoms that you do. Pray for the house churches in Cuba; give to a group that assists the persecuted indigenous Church in Vietnam; find a way to assist the leaders of the underground Church who are presently in prison in China. Express your gratitude to God for His blessings in your life by specifically remembering other Christians who are in great danger. Allow your generous goodness to bear fruit in the lives of your persecuted brothers and sisters.

4. Care specifically for widows and orphans, following the biblical examples from Zechariah and James. Adopt a nursing home or a children's home and begin providing for these special people through your prayers, your time, and your assets. Be a Big Brother or Big Sister for a child with one or no parents. Notice the widows in your life and treat one to lunch or to a walk through a garden or a park. Give yourself in goodness.

5. Give away something that you really value or that is important to you. Give it away for no other reason than to prevent greed from setting into your heart. Give away a car or a piece of jewelry or a special book or collectible. Give it to charity, to a friend, to your child or sibling. Give it to your church. Experience the sheer freedom of giving and the joy of goodness blossoming in your heart.

FAITHFULNESS

". . . the fruit of the Spirit is love, joy, peace, patience, kindness, generosity, FAITHFULNESS, gentleness, self-control . . ." Galatians 5:22–23

Faithfulness

7. A WORD WITH
GREAT ANCESTORS

God says go. And Abraham does just that. He goes.

Faithfulness comes from good stock. If ever a word had good parents, impressive grandparents, and sterling ancestors, it is *faithfulness*. That's because *faithfulness* comes from God Himself.

God. The God who made a covenant with Abraham and said, "I will be faithful to you." God. The same God who made a covenant with Moses and the Israelites and said, "I will be faithful to you." God. The very God who made a covenant with the entire world by sending Jesus Christ in order to say, "In Him, I am faithful to you." God is faithful. That means God keeps His word. God does what He says He will do. He makes good on His promises. God is true even when His people are not. Faithfulness is an old, old word. Faithfulness is a good word. It is God's word.

Maybe it is because it is such an old word that *faithfulness* seems so hopelessly old-fashioned and outdated anymore. Most American marriages end in divorce. Nearly half of American babies are born to unwed mothers, if they are born at all. The idea of faithfulness has lost favor. We make vows to lovers and spouses, promises to children, friends, and coworkers and then fail to follow through with them. More American adults today believe that it is acceptable to be unfaithful to one's spouse, to commit adultery, than ever before in our history. Faithfulness seems like a relic, a thing of the past. Our celebrities revel in their unfaithfulness, appearing with a new boyfriend this week, moving in with him the following week, and then appearing again in a few months in yet another new relationship. Meanwhile, the media celebrates their desire to be "happy," all the while forgetting that faithfulness to God and faithfulness to one another may indeed be the way to happiness and life itself.

Faithfulness is of God. He is the author of faithfulness, and He made you to be faithful. In fact, it is only when you learn the depths of His faithfulness that you will become the-best-version-of-yourself. God has expectations for us. When we are faithful to His expectations, the blessings of God can be remarkable.

Faithfulness is a fruit of God's Spirit because God is faithful to us. With the Holy Spirit's help, you will grow in faithfulness and your heart will take on an entirely new dimension and character. Your faithfulness will begin to reflect the faithfulness of God.

God's Faithfulness

The Bible story that has impacted me most is, without question, the story of the ninety-nine-year-old man named Abraham. God chooses Abraham to be the father of God's very own people. He tells Abraham, "I will make of you a great nation." God never gives the reason why He chooses Abraham. He simply chooses Abraham and tells him to go wherever God leads. Remarkably, God never provides much detail as to where Abraham will go, only that he should follow God's lead. God is in charge, not Abraham. And He instructs Abraham to move to an unnamed land that God will eventually show him (Gen. 12:1–4).

Very simply, God teaches Abraham about faith. In essence, God is saying, "Trust me, and all the other details will be taken care of. If you trust me, I will be faithful." From the moment of God's choosing Abraham, the rest of the entire Bible tells the story of God's faithfulness to that very first promise to Abraham. That promise is God's promise to you: "If you trust me, I will be faithful."

Recall the words of that divine promise.

*The Lord said to Abram, "**Go** forth from the land of your kinsfolk and from your father's house **to a land that I will show you.***

I will make of you a great nation, and I will bless you;

I will make your name great, so that you will be a blessing.

I will bless those who bless you

and curse those who curse you.

All the communities of the earth shall find blessing in you."

Abram went as the Lord directed him*. . . .*
(Gen. 12:1–4a)

God says go. And Abraham does just that. He goes.

Later, in case Abraham worries and frets, God says, *"Fear not, Abram! I am your shield; I will make your reward very great."* (Gen. 15:1) God promises to give Abraham and Sarah a son even though they are well into their nineties and have not yet produced a child in their marriage. This promised son will be the beginning of God's chosen people forever. Surely God must be crazy! Children to a barren couple in their nineties? *"God brought Abraham outside and said, 'Look toward heaven, and **count the stars** if you are able to count them. **So shall your descendants be.**'"* (Gen. 15:5 [NRSV])

Then, in Genesis 17, after Abraham has followed and obeyed God's direction to reach the unnamed land, God spells out His promises in even more detail. In sum, God tells Abraham, "This is my covenant with you:

1) You will be the **ancestor** of a multitude of nations.

2) Your **name** shall be changed from Abram to Abraham.

3) I will make you exceedingly **fruitful**.

4) This will be an **everlasting** covenant.

5) I will give to you, and to your offspring after you, the **land** where you are now an alien, all the land of Canaan, for a **perpetual holding.**

6) **I will be their God.**

7) In return, you and your offspring will **circumcise** every male."

This one chapter of Genesis establishes the foundation for everything that occurs in the Bible from this point onward. God's faithfulness to the promise is staggering and wonderful! He provides the promised child to the elderly barren couple with the birth of Isaac, who becomes the father of Jacob, Israel. And that birth paves the way for the stories of Jacob and Esau; the saga of Joseph and his brothers; the gift of Moses, who leads the Exodus of the people of Israel out of Egypt and into the promised land; the leadership of Joshua, the Judges, Saul, David, and Solomon; and the words of truth from the prophets. Over and over again, the Old Testament records God's faithfulness to Israel.

In the New Testament, God then extends His covenant with Abraham beyond Israel to the entire world through the gift of God's own son, Jesus. Because God is faithful through the ages, Abraham becomes your father and mine when we become believers in Jesus. Saint Paul tells us, *"It is those who have faith who are children of Abraham. . . . Consequently, those who have faith are blessed along with Abraham who had faith."* (Gal. 3:7–9). God's promise to Abraham becomes God's promise to you because God is faithful. Trust God and He will be faithful.

God makes a simple covenant promise to Abraham and proves

His faithfulness all the way through the Bible, through history, and into your life! God is indeed faithful and true. Faithfulness is simply part of God's character; it's who He is. And if God is faithful, those who live in His Spirit will be faithful. You will be known for your faithfulness.

Faithful to the End: Matthew 25:14–30

When you arrive in Matthew 25, Jesus is nearing the end of His time on earth. His ministry with the disciples is drawing to a close, and He is preparing to face the cross. In these last days together, Jesus teaches them that the end will come when they least expect it, and that they need to be ready because He will come again in glory to judge all the world. Jesus's point is plain: He instructs His disciples and followers to be faithful, to be about the business that God made them for and to set aside the things that are not of God. To be faithful means to tend to the work that God created you for. Only when you pursue faithfulness to God can you become the-best-version-of-yourself.

Remember the parable of the talents (Matthew 25:14–30) discussed earlier in the study. Now let's take another look at this powerful parable from the perspective of faithfulness. Jesus tells you about a wealthy man who leaves for a long journey. Before he leaves, the man entrusts three of his servants with large sums of money. He entrusts the first servant with five talents (about $2 million in today's dollars), the second servant with two talents (about $800,000), and the third servant with one talent (about $400,000). Once the master leaves, each of the servants is on his own until he returns from his journey. The first two servants work, invest, and trade the money given to them. As a result, they double their investments. Out of fear, the third servant digs a hole in the ground and hides his master's money so that he is sure not to lose any of it.

After a long time, the master returns and inquires as to what each of the servants has done with the money he has entrusted to them. When he learns that the first servant has turned five talents into ten and the second servant has turned two talents into four, the master rejoices. To each of these two men, the wealthy man says, *"Well done, my good and **faithful** servant. Since you were **faithful** in small matters, I will give you great responsibilities. Come, share your master's joy."*

But when the master discovers that the third servant has done nothing more than bury his money and delivers no return or interest at all, he rebukes the servant, calls him "worthless," and casts him out of the Kingdom altogether.

There are lots of things to notice about this parable. First, the master entrusts huge sums of money to his servants. In Jesus's time, servants often had tremendous amounts of freedom, particularly to do business on behalf of their master. In fact, it was not uncommon for an owner to entrust nearly all of his business affairs and wealth to a handful of competent, business-savvy servants.

Second, the master clearly expects a return on his investment. He wants his servants to manage his wealth, not merely bury it. He expects that a faithful servant will grow what he has been given. When the master returns, he has a day of reckoning or accounting with his servants. He intends for his servants to be about the business of managing what he has entrusted to them.

Third, the master generously rewards the two servants who produce a return. He praises them for their faithfulness. Because they have been faithful in this venture, the master gives them even more to manage and to tend. He must be marvelously wealthy, for he calls the sums he entrusted to the three servants merely "a few things." Only the absurdly wealthy would consider three million dollars small. How much more did he entrust to those two faithful servants?

What does this tell you about God? A lot.

1) **God is absurdly wealthy.** In fact, all creation belongs to Him. *"The earth is the Lord's and all it holds."* (Ps. 24:1) Everything you see, possess, or touch belongs to Him. It is not yours or anyone else's. God alone is the source. The world belongs to God. He made it and merely entrusts a portion of it to you for a short while. You may be a manager, a steward, or a servant while you are here, but make no mistake, God is the owner, the source, and the master. God possesses; you and I merely manage.

2) **God is a Giver. God gives you at least four things:**

Time: Every moment and day is a gift from Him. He is the Author of Life.

Money and Possessions: All that you have is a gift from the Source, God. It is not yours. You merely manage it while you are here. When you die, God hands those resources and possessions to someone else. And you are judged based on what you did with them while they were under your management.

Talents: God invests skills, gifts, and abilities in each human being. Some receive musical gifts, while others receive athletic skills; some are gifted with craftsmanship, while still others have intellectual abilities. You do not earn those; you merely receive them from God. What you do with those gifts is your gift to God. But the gifts themselves come from Him.

Faith: God instills within each person a deep sense of who He is. Remember Saint Augustine's prayer, "Our hearts are restless until they rest in You, O Lord." You may hide it, deny it, or run from it, but deep within you is the precious God-given gift of faith. God invites you to believe and to follow Him just like Abraham did.

3) **God expects a return on His investment in you.** God does not gift you with life, time, money, talents, and faith for no reason. Quite the contrary. God expects, like the master in the parable, that you will utilize and manage all that He has given you to produce a return for Him.

What does that return look like? Jesus gives two primary examples. In His final words to His disciples, Jesus gives them their great commission: *"Go, therefore, and **make disciples** of all nations, baptizing them in the name of the Father, and of the Son, and of the Holy Spirit, teaching them to **observe all that I have commanded** you."* (Mt. 28:19–20).

God expects each of us to use our gifts to make disciples: to share the good news and the Word, and to help lives to be changed by the Gospel. God desires for the world to believe in Jesus Christ, to call Him Lord, and to follow Him. As a result, God expects His gifts to you to help make that Kingdom mission happen. That is the return on investment. Your faithfulness in using your gifts will result in changed hearts, saved souls, new lives, and transformed relationships. Saint Alphonsus Liguori put it this way: "I love Jesus Christ and that is why I am on fire with the desire to give Him souls, first of all my own, and then an incalculable number of others."

Second, Jesus again points out that God expects His followers to care for the least, the last, and the lost. In fact, Jesus goes so far as to say that at the judgment God will note how you have cared for the naked, the hungry, the thirsty, the imprisoned, the stranger, and the sick (Mt. 25:31–46). Jesus points this out in the very next teachings after He shares the parable of the talents in Matthew 25:14–30.

God's heart seeks to heal the wounds of the world, and God's people will too. Your faithfulness will produce healed wounds, mended hurts, and quenched appetites.

Very simply, God wants, expects, and desires His followers to love Him completely and to love our neighbors as we love ourselves. And to use every resource that He has invested in you to do so! That leads you to become the-best-version-of-yourself.

4) **God encourages boldness and risk-taking.** The master is not pleased in the parable with the servant who merely buries his investment in the ground and lives in fear. God encourages you to take risks to share His love and to be bold in binding up the wounds of your neighbors. There is no such thing as a passive follower of Jesus. Followers follow! Following takes effort, and it may involve bold risks. In fact, it is a sin (sloth) to be unwilling to venture out and act with what God has given us. Sloth sits idly by and wastes the gifts of God. Sloth cannot muster enough love to do anything for anyone. Sloth is the-worst-version-of-yourself: lazy, indifferent, and passive. God has invested vast amounts in you, and He expects you to be faithful.

5) **Jesus will return to "settle accounts."** The day is coming when we shall see Jesus face-to-face, when God will evaluate you for how you have managed His investment of time, money, talents, and faith. Make no mistake: You and I will ultimately answer for just how faithful we have been. Have we lived boldly and invested God's gifts or have we lived fearfully and done nothing? That is why it is called the Judgment Day. Jesus will return and sit in judgment over us.

6) **Excuses are not accepted.** The third servant had lots of good reasons for why he failed to produce a return for God. He was scared; he was conservative. What he failed to understand was

that no excuse is satisfactory. This is what we were made for: to love God and to fulfill His mission in the world. No excuse exists because there is nothing else to do but to serve God. All else is but a shadow fading away. Our faithfulness is life itself.

The Examples of Caj and Phyllis

Anita and I met Father Caj when we were living in Connecticut and I was attending graduate school. Neither of us had spent much time around Catholic priests before, but my graduate work introduced us to some new friends. Fr. Caj was eighty-nine years old when we met him, and I was a not yet thirty-year-old graduate student looking to get out of New England as quickly as I could. Our hearts were in Georgia and in the life God had for us there. We viewed our time in Connecticut as but a short period of preparation for what God had in store for us in the future. That view was more correct than we could ever have imagined.

Fr. Caj lived with a group of Dominican friars, one of whom studied with me, tutored me, enjoyed dinner with our family, and became our dear family friend. Fr. Caj had "retired" from the parish ministry of pastoring and had transitioned into a new ministry of prayer. Each morning and each evening, he and the other priests gathered for prayer. Most attended as they could based on their duties, but Fr. Caj was always there.

Occasionally, I would stop by the priory where the priests lived after my classes just to visit and to check in with my classmate. The priory was directly on my route when walking back to our house from my classes. Anita and I were a long way from home, and with no one checking on us, the priests became our family in Connecticut. Although we were Methodists at the time, several of the priests embraced our family as if we were their own. They understood better than I that we are all kin.

More often than not, when I stopped by the priory on my way home, I would enter the little chapel for some quiet time before I walked the rest of the way back to our house. Each time I saw a number of different priests, but I always saw Fr. Caj.

Fr. Caj was a curmudgeon, an old New Englander in every way—a bit crotchety, full of opinions and not afraid to share them. However, without fail, each time I saw him, Fr. Caj asked about my health, which was not good at the time. He asked about my wife, who was struggling to care for our daughters as I struggled with illness and classes, and he asked about my children. Every time. Without fail. And each time, without fail, he would say in his ornery New England Catholic priest kind of way, "Well, I've been praying for all of you." And I knew those were not empty words. They were heartfelt and deeply true. After all, Fr. Caj practically lived in the prayer chapel. His was a life devoted to prayer. Faithfulness.

Fr. Caj had spent sixty years pastoring churches before he retired to this ministry of prayer. When he retired, the secretaries at his new church home and priory always knew that if someone needed a pastor in an emergency, Fr. Caj was the one to call. Even late at night or early on Christmas morning, he was always ready, always willing, and always eager to go. At eighty-nine years of age. Still faithful, like the polestar—true north, always.

When I met him, Fr. Caj still wore the same clothes he had been wearing for nearly thirty years. Each month, he took his small pension and placed it in its entirety in the Poor Box, the small box at the front of the church where believers could give to help ease the pain of those around them. He bought no new clothes. The parish where he lived provided the food and shelter he actually needed, and Fr. Caj figured that was enough. So he gave all that he had. At eighty-nine years old. Still faithful, still true.

I will always remember one special day when I stopped by to pray and ran into Fr. Caj. I knew he had been in continuous prayer for a friend of ours. When I saw him, his head was swollen with a large bruise. "Fr. Caj, what happened?" I asked. His chest expanded with a small bit of pride. He chuckled and replied, "Oh, I was in the prayer chapel, and I was praying for you. I fell asleep and hit my head on the railing." He rubbed his hand over his bandaged forehead as if it were a red badge of prayer courage. Fr. Caj was the first person I've ever known who was wounded in prayer. Faithfulness.

Fr. Caj radiated a deep loyalty to Christ that comes only with time. That loyalty had grown Fr. Caj's faithfulness to a level that few of us can hope to attain. He lived for Christ, to love Him and to love His people. Fr. Caj exhibited faithfulness in nearly every aspect of his life: faithful in prayer, faithful in generous and sacrificial giving, faithful in a life of eager and joyful service. Clearly, Fr. Caj and Jesus were good friends. The faithfulness of God flowed so deeply in Fr. Caj's veins that it nearly oozed out of his pores. Fr. Caj was faithful and true because God is faithful and true, always.

Phyllis understood that also. Phyllis was an elderly woman in our congregation who created a ministry with babies and their families. Her heart overflowed with a love for God's smallest children. Phyllis's eyes lit up when she saw a baby; her eyes sparkled when she held that child. Well into her eighties, week in and week out, Phyllis ministered to the smallest among us by rocking children and caring for them in the nursery during worship. She developed her own special prayer team to pray for each child who was baptized as well as for that child's family. She wrote the families prayer cards; she hosted a breakfast each year for all the babies baptized in the preceding year and their parents to celebrate God's faithful grace in their lives.

At her advanced age, however, Phylllis's body began to experience the breakdowns and challenges that come naturally with aging. Her walk became slow and laborious, requiring the assistance of a cane. Her body simply did not want to cooperate with her spirit. With every passing Sunday, it grew increasingly difficult for her simply to arrive at the nursery.

So you can imagine our amazement one stormy Sunday morning as we prepared for worship around eight a.m. As leaders, we had resigned ourselves to the fact that very few would attend church that day given the rains and wind. It seemed obvious that most folks would awaken, hear the rain, and just roll over to stay in the comfort of a warm, dry bed.

As we looked out the window and prayed for that Sunday's worship, a small car arrived and settled into the handicapped parking area. Slowly but surely, a woman emerged from the car, first cracking open the door, then opening an umbrella, and finally stepping out of her seat and onto the pavement. Slowly but surely, elderly Phyllis made her way into the nursery in the pouring rain on a day when many folks far younger and healthier would not muster the spirit to worship God. But Phyllis knew and knows her calling. She loved God, and she loved God's children. She never considered anything else. Because Phyllis is faithful as God is faithful.

Right there before our very eyes, Phyllis was displaying every bit of the-best-version-of-herself. In pain. In the rain. Devoted to love. Faithful.

The-best-version-of-yourself will be faithful to the purposes and gifts given you by God.

GROWING A LIFE OF FAITHFULNESS

1. Set measurable goals. What do you think that God wants you to do with your life? God's dream for you may be that you are a godly mother, or an earner of money to be invested for His mission, or that you teach with a holy passion. Establish three to five goals that reflect the return you think God desires from your life. Some of these may be family related, some may be professional, and some may be personal. Reflect on how you can use your time, talents, money, and faith to generate these results. What can you do this week to help make it happen? Write down a goal for each area of your life for the coming year and sketch out a plan for how to achieve that goal.

2. Claim the strengths and gifts that God has uniquely invested in you. God wants you to use them for His Kingdom. Don't try to imitate or claim the gifts of others. God made you the way you are for a reason. Claim those gifts and strengths and use them for Him. He will be faithful when you do. By making a list, you can begin to pray for specifics on how He most wants you to use what He has invested in you.

3. Remember whom you serve in everything you do for one day. Begin each day with the simple prayer that God will enable you to serve Him with your gifts for that one day. Remember: God is the Source. He gave the gifts. God is the Owner and the Master. You serve Him. Never be seduced into thinking that your gifts belong to you: They are God's. Never be tempted to use your gifts for your gain or glory: They are for God's Kingdom and glory. Serve Him faithfully in all that you do, and you will be amazed.

4. Memorize Mother Teresa's encouragement: "God did not call you to be successful; He calls you to be faithful."

5. Embrace simple faithfulness in financial affairs. Live the famous Christian saying, "Earn all you can. Save all you can. Give all you can." Being faithful in your finances will multiply itself into every area of your life in ways you will never expect. Three guidelines, suggested by John Wesley, a Protestant contemporary of Saint Alphonsus Liguori, will help you do just that.

> A. *Earn all you can* (1 Tim. 6:17–18): Do so without giving your heart away to your income and pursuits. Your heart belongs to God alone.
>
> > • Do not sacrifice your body, mind, or health.
> >
> > • Do not do so at the expense of your neighbor.
> >
> > • Use honest, hard work.
>
> B. *Save all you can* (Hb. 13:5): Simplicity is a virtue.
>
> > • Don't seek to satisfy your every whim or fancy.
> >
> > • Don't squander what you have on expensive, frivolous stuff.
> >
> > • Know that the more your passions are indulged, the more they will increase.
> >
> > • Don't weigh yourself down with stuff.
> >
> > • Seek not to impress others but simply to provide for your and your family's needs.
>
> C. *Give all you can* (2 Cor. 9:6–8): Use your possessions faithfully to love God and to love people. .
>
> > • You are a steward, not an owner; it all belongs to God.
> >
> > • Provide for your and your family's needs.

- Then give all that you can. Do not confine yourself to a number: ten percent, one-third, or even half: Give all that you can.

- Good questions to ask yourself when considering spending money:

  1) Am I acting like a steward of the Lord's goods?

  2) Can I offer this expense as a sacrifice to God through Jesus?

  3) Do I think that this will generate God's favor at my resurrection judgment?

GENTLENESS

*"... the fruit of the Spirit is love, joy, peace,
patience, kindness, generosity, faithfulness,
GENTLENESS, self-control ..."*
Galatians 5:22–23

Gentleness

8. YOUR SECRET WEAPON

That's why Saint Bernard of Clairvaux taught that the four keys to your faith are "humility, humility, humility, humility."

Anger. Temper.

You just are not very pretty when you're angry and out of control, are you? You're off the chain, veins popping, eyes bulging, face turning red. It's hard to be the-best-version-of-yourself when you look like that.

To be honest, when I meet someone with an explosive temper, I usually try my best to avoid that person. Tempers are scary, even dangerous. And explosive tempers especially do not look good on Christians.

That does not mean, however, that Christians should be pushovers or pansies. Quite the contrary: Christians are strong and courageous. When you know who you are and to whom you belong, a gentle strength flows out of that knowledge. Why? Because gentleness flows from the strong, bold Spirit of God. Gentleness is a sign of strength, not weakness, in the same way that bullying is a sign of weakness, not strength. Christians are free to be gentle because we live for a purpose higher than merely getting our own way in this world. Instead, believers get satisfaction and pleasure in seeking and knowing God's way rather than our own.

If gentleness is a fruit of God's Spirit, and the-best-version-of-yourself will be gentle, how does the Bible help grow gentleness? In four ways.

Four Qualities of Biblical Gentleness

1) Being at ease

First of all, the-best-version-of-yourself is at ease, with yourself and with God. To know Jesus Christ is to be made right with God. You quit trying to do things your way and you begin to obey God's way. You can never be gentle until you are right with God. You will always fight within yourself and with your own desires. In Christ, you begin to live life as it is intended. Jesus puts you at ease with the Lord. And then you can be at ease with yourself. And then you can be gentle. The inner tensions are calmed.

Christians experience ease because the stresses and tensions of living are relieved by the Spirit of God. When you are operating on your own strength, you are tense, uptight, and struggling. Things are never quite right. Nothing feels settled. But when you are living in the Spirit of God, operating on His strength and His agenda, you find a relaxing freedom in knowing that you are living in His will rather than your own. The worries and tension fade away. Gentleness is the result.

Saint Paul provides this basic encouragement in Romans 8:31b: *"If God is for us, who can be against us?"* When we are on God's side, many of our worries and fears fade away. In the end, we realize that we are His. We belong to Him and we can trust Him for what lies ahead, including today. He stands with us. Tensions decrease. Gentleness results. You are free to be gentle and at ease because you know that God stands with you.

The New Testament Greek word for "gentleness" literally means "to have a tamed neck." What a great image! Mules exemplify a stubborn, resistant neck. That captures how we live before we are in Christ. Before Christ, we fight and resist, always struggling against our untamed passions and habits. Or we struggle with the annoyances or demands of other people. Some folks are controlled by anger and addictions, others by depression and despair. Some obsessively seek the admiration and praise of other people and end up hopelessly enslaved to their need for approval. Before Christ, we are not at ease. We are restless, stubborn, and resistant.

However, once you are in Christ, you begin to be tamed and settled. Stubbornness and resistance subside so that gentleness can emerge. Your spirit now cooperates with the Spirit of God. Instead of finding tension and harshness in continually fighting against God, you now find the gentleness of obeying Him and walking in His way. Rather than straining to seek the approval of others, you have been approved by God. You are at ease. That is what you were made for in the first place: the-best-version-of-yourself.

Fr. Brian may be the most settled, gentle person I have ever known. I became friends with him at a monastery where I spend a day in prayer each month. Fr. Brian leads that monastery as abbot. For a time, he agreed to meet with me periodically for spiritual friendship, conversation, and guidance. On most occasions, after leaving my pastoral work and waging battle through an hour's worth of traffic, I would arrive frazzled, tense about the world's worries. Stubborn and resistant toward God because I was consumed by the world. And each time I would find Brian completely at ease and greeting me with a divine calmness. Through years of prayer, devotion, leadership, and service, the Holy Spirit has so invaded Fr. Brian's life that everything about him radiates a sense of being at ease. Patiently listening to me, calmly smiling, and faithfully praying with me, Fr. Brian would inevitably stir a gentleness within me that had not existed before. His gentleness could reach deep within me to pull out the ease that God has in mind. His gentle ease led me closer to Jesus.

2) Self-control

The-best-version-of-yourself keeps your anger and your passion under control. The-best-version-of-yourself is not controlled by overeating or by an obsession with continually acquiring more worldly stuff. In this way, gentleness partners with the fruit of self-control. The Spirit brings control. The Spirit does not produce explosive, out-of-control, violent, scary people. God's Spirit does not lead to the overindulgence of every fleshly whim or emotional desire.

For example, think about anger. Anger is not always bad. There are times when you are right to be angry. When criminals attack innocent victims, or when a child is abused, anger is a justifiable reaction. However, anger can easily cross into dangerous territory when it seeks to hurt others or to avenge. A Christian's anger, even when it is righteous, is always tempered with love and mercy. Out-of-control anger is sin. Anger may occasionally be justifiable; sin is not.

One of the most unpleasant experiences in my life came when I had no choice but to serve in a ministry alongside a person whose anger was out of control. His explosiveness and rage in every situation demoralized volunteers and created a sense of fear throughout the ministry. Anyone who served or shared in that ministry was terrified of being the victim of one of his outbursts or tantrums. Sadly, over time, his lack of gentleness slowly squeezed the joy and the purpose out of that ministry. Worse than his lack of gentleness was his lack of self-control to allow gentleness to emerge in his soul.

In contrast, Christians control their passions rather than allowing their passions to control them. Only the Holy Spirit can make that possible, because the Bible is clear that before you are a Christian, you can't help but be a slave to your passions. Listen to Ephesians 2:3: *"All of us once lived . . . in the desires of our flesh, following the wishes of the flesh and the impulses . . ."* In other words, before you embraced Jesus, you gave in to your passions and desires. Now you give in to Christ and His Spirit. We gain control through the Spirit of gentleness.

3) Humility

Humility is the first cousin of gentleness. They go hand in hand. When your pride is held in check and your ego is contained, humility results. Humility lives at the heart of God. That's why Saint Bernard of Clairvaux taught that the four keys to your faith are "humility, humility, humility, humility."

Humility remembers that other people matter just as much as you do. God loves each one of us just the same. Whether we are rich or poor, young or old, handsome or homely, God loves us immeasurably and equally. That one basic fact builds the foundation of humility. Say it aloud: "I am just as valuable to God as any other person." Now say this: "Any other person is just as important to God as I am."

We are arrogant when we view ourselves too highly and others too poorly. No gentleness resides there—only pride. And pride forms humility's arch nemesis. That means C. S. Lewis was right when he said that pride is the supreme anti-God state of mind. To combat that deadly sin, humility emerges from knowing who we are: a child loved by God.

Humility leads directly to gentleness. Gentleness is not proud or puffed up. Gentleness treats other people like we want to be treated in return. A gentle believer cares as much about his neighbor as he does about himself. Gentleness seeks humbly to make other people look better. A gentle Christian sincerely and earnestly seeks the best for the other people around her. Most important, gentleness seeks God's salvation for others.

Gentleness is particularly important as you share your faith with nonbelievers. A harsh, judgmental spirit will usually result in rejection and dismissal. Perhaps that's why Saint Paul reminds us in 2 Tim. 2:24–25: *"A slave of the Lord should not quarrel, but should be gentle with everyone, able to teach, tolerant, correcting opponents with kindness. It may be that God will grant them repentance that leads to knowledge of the truth."*

A gentle spirit allows others to approach you, to hear the truth, and to ask questions. Harshness and severity close off the conversation too soon. Gentleness creates room for people around you to come and meet Jesus through you. Harshness slams the door quickly. Cultivating a gentle spirit will bear fruit for God's Kingdom in the lives of people around you.

4) Forgiveness

Finally, gentleness roots itself in forgiveness. Gentle believers do not hold grudges. Instead, they are molded by the hand of the Lord, who is forgiving and gentle. Once you realize just how much God has forgiven you, it is hard not to reflect that same forgiveness to the people in your life. A humble self-awareness of your own sins then leads to a growing ability to forgive others. *That* is gentleness of spirit. The-best-version-of-yourself does not treat others harshly while asking God to treat you gently. Quite the contrary: The closer you are drawn to God, the more forgiving and gentle you will become.

Now, that is very different from a world that seeks vengeance and rejects forgiveness. We live in an unforgiving, grudge-holding world. For example, the Scottish government opened a $4.5 million visitor center at Glencoe, where 310 years ago, members of the Campbell clan slaughtered thirty-eight members of the MacDonald clan. When the site opened, Roddy Campbell was introduced as the center's director. An angry Hector MacDonald responded to the announcement of Mr. Campbell's appointment by saying to reporters, "Don't get me wrong. I have nothing against the Campbells, but I would not stay a night in the company of one." The news reporter covering the story wrote, "There are still some very strong feelings about the massacre here." What an understatement! More than ten generations have passed, but members of these two families still cling to a 310-year-old grudge. That may be a world record for grudge holding. And where grudge holding reigns, gentleness cannot grow.

However, while the world may be harsh, bitter, and cynical, the believer gently extends the hand of forgiveness and the spirit of gentleness. Christians may be in the world, but they always know that they are not *of* it.

My children have taught me this lesson better than anyone else. Their ability to forgive, and even to forget, regularly amazes me. When I am harsh or sharp tongued, they are quick to forgive me gently and move forward. They release their grudges rather than bear the weight of carrying them. My elder daughter routinely points out to us, her parents, what she calls "the two most helpful words" in the English language when she reminds us, "Nobody's perfect." My own two daughters' witness explains to me in part why Jesus tells us to receive the Kingdom like children. Gentleness and forgiveness often come easily to them.

Yet, adults can embody the gentleness of forgiveness too. Do you remember the story of Joseph and his brothers in Genesis? Joseph's brothers are so jealous of his gifts and abilities that they sell him into slavery to get rid of him. They hate Joseph because their father loves him most. After he is sold, over time, the slave Joseph rises to power under the pharaoh in Egypt. After decades of separation, his brothers come to Egypt to ask for help and relief from a famine that is starving their land to death. When they meet Joseph, they have no idea who he is. They think they are asking the key leader of Egypt for aid, but because it has been a long time since they've seen Joseph, they fail to recognize him. At last, after all these years, Joseph finally has his chance for revenge. Remarkably, rather than getting even for an old grudge, Joseph instead offers his betraying brothers a full measure of forgiveness.

Joseph has grown so close to the Lord that he is able to see God's hand at work in every aspect of his life, even in his brothers' selling him into slavery. God has shaped his spirit with such a gentleness that Joseph is able to tell his brothers, *"So it was not really you but God who had me come here; and he has made of me a father to Pharaoh, lord of all his household, and ruler over the whole land of Egypt."* (Gen. 45:8)

Joseph combines his forgiveness with generosity. He provides for his brothers and their families, giving them food and shelter during their time of suffering and famine (Gen. 45:11). Despite all of this gentleness, his brothers later still worry that Joseph will not be able to forgive them (Gen. 50:15). And Joseph again amazes them with his spirit of gentleness. *"Even though you meant harm to me, God meant it for good to achieve his present end, the survival of many people. Therefore, have no fear; I will provide for you and for your children."* (Gen. 50:20) The trust in God in that passage still astonishes me.

Joseph is proof that God's Spirit brings a gentleness that expresses itself in forgiveness as well as in generosity.

This same spirit of gentleness can take root in you as well. When you discover the misdeeds or failures of a brother or sister in Christ, God calls you to seek to restore rather than reject that friend in Christ. *"Brothers, even if a person is caught in some transgression, you who are spiritual should correct that one in a gentle spirit."* (Gal. 6:1)

Rejection is easy. Restoration is hard work. Joseph shows us the way as he faces his brothers years after their betrayal of him. He does so with gentleness, grace, mercy, and love. Clearly, restoration and healing are possible only through God. God's Spirit alone can provide that kind of healing and forgiveness. God wants to mold you into a person of gentle forgiveness. God desires for you to be the-best-version-of-yourself.

Gentleness Helps People Find Their Way Home

"Sanctify Christ as Lord in your hearts. Always be ready to give an explanation to anyone who asks you for a reason for your hope, but do it with **gentleness and reverence.** (1 Peter 3:15–16)

In this passage, Saint Peter makes your aim clear: holy hearts, hearts made holy by Christ. *That* is the-best-version-of-yourself. Holy hearts with a God-given hope. And Peter also makes it clear that your gentleness can help other people meet your Lord, Jesus Christ. What an opportunity: to have your own gentleness help lead others to salvation. That is a truly Christian way of looking at gentleness.

Too often, the world is full of arrogant, self-righteous Christians who are smug and secure in their own salvation and ever so eager to point out the sins of the people around them, like the Christian who listens to sermons so that he can tell others how good they ought to be while never looking at himself in the mirror. Or the Christian who sees herself as the world's police officer, patrolling the globe hoping to point out everyone else's wrongs. In these verses, Saint Peter clearly envisions just the opposite. A Christian is a gentle person who loves others and graciously shares what she has, especially her hope in Christ. That is who Christians are: humble, caring people with holy hearts that love God. Holy hearts rooted in gentleness.

Don is a highly effective evangelist, although he would never consider himself as such. He is no professional; he is not a priest, nor does he ever preach from pulpits. Instead, when the opportunity presents itself, Don gently tells the people around him about Jesus. He allows the Holy Spirit to make him a gentle person, easily approached and readily befriended. Don seeks to meet people where they are. He relates to the people in his neighborhood, in his workplace, and in his relationships in a way that is warm and inviting. Don never argues about the truth; rather, he patiently listens to the other person's thoughts. After listening, he reflects and gently replies with the truth of the faith. Don responds to confrontation with a smile and an outstretched hand. He allows gentleness to carry the day. He hopes to be loving more than to be right.

Don is no pushover; on the contrary, he is quite firm in who he is and what he believes. He stands with the Church. But the reason that hundreds of people around him have come to faith in Christ is because of his gentleness. Quite simply, Don carries a gentle heart that loves people, and he remembers his God-given opportunity: to let his gentleness lead other people to the living waters of Jesus.

The Gentleness Model of Jesus

For a model of gentleness, of course, Jesus provides the supreme example. Consider the events of His ministry. Discover the awesome power and strength that lie beneath His gentleness.

Walk with Jesus through the Gospel of Luke as He:

- Touches and heals a leper who desperately begs to be delivered from a deadly disease that prevents other people from touching or even associating with him (5:12–16).

- Teaches His followers to "…love your enemies, do good to those who hate you, bless those who curse you, pray for those who mistreat you." (6:27–31)

- Consoles a widow whose son has just died and then brings the boy back to life (7:11–17).

- Rebukes the Pharisee who chastises the well-known sinful woman as she kisses and anoints Jesus's feet. Jesus then forgives her sins and sends her forth with His blessing (7:36–50).

- Demonstrates to His arguing disciples where true greatness lies by embracing and welcoming a small child (9:46–48).

- Tells the parable of the good Samaritan, whose gentleness, generosity, and mercy overflowed and for which he expected no repayment. Note how Jesus tells the lawyer, "Go and do likewise." (10:25–37)

- Lays hands on a woman who has been crippled for eighteen years, even though the religious leaders criticize His doing so on the Sabbath (13:10–17).

- Welcomes the little children whom His own disciples are

turning away (18:15–17).

- Endures His trial before Pilate and Herod, His humiliation in front of the crowd, and His death on the cross (23:1–43).

- Instructs the women weeping by the side of the road as He walks the agonizing way to Calvary, saying to them, "Do not weep for me; weep instead for yourselves and for your children." (23:28)

- Loves even the two criminals dying on either side of Him at the cross. Listen as He says to the believing one, "Amen, I say to you, today you will be with me in Paradise." (23:43)

The strength and power of Jesus emerge full force in His gentleness. Jesus faces His enemies with gentleness. He encounters the weak and the outcast with gentleness. His courage provides the platform for an extraordinary outpouring of gentleness even when He is suffering and at the point of death.

Contrary to popular opinion, gentleness has tremendous power. Of course it does—it is a fruit of God's Spirit. And there is no power like that of the Holy Spirit.

Come, Holy Spirit, come. Fill our lives with your power and your gentleness. Help us become gentle and forgiving: the-best-version-of-ourselves.

GROWING A LIFE OF GENTLENESS

1. Learn to count to ten. That may be the single greatest step in learning to control your anger and your temper. When your emotional temperature rises, when the temptation to lash out is strongest, learn to count to ten to allow yourself the time and space to back off. Let gentleness slowly replace anger and impulse. Your first instinct may not be your best. Learning to count may well be your most productive way to grow in gentleness.

2. Exercise. Simple but true: Regular, rigorous exercise releases endorphins in your body. These agents calm your body and still your mind and soul. A calmer body and soul provide fertile ground for gentleness to grow.

3. Write a letter of forgiveness or make restitution for damages caused in order to eliminate the grudges you still hold as well as those held against you. Old hurts and wounds have a remarkable power over us. They build up like water behind a dam, slowly increasing over time to a level that can no longer be held back. Take the difficult steps to mend old hurts. Initiate the first step. Write a letter to forgive or to seek forgiveness. If the person is now dead, write the letter anyway. It will cleanse you and set you free to treat others gently rather than harshly. If you have hurt someone or something, find a way to make restitution. Pay back the debt in some way. Remove the bonds and shackles that prevent you from living with gentleness.

4. Volunteer in the nursery of your church. Play with a baby. Spend time with the vulnerable and the innocent so that the Spirit of gentleness can stir deep within you. Tom is a disabled man, frustrated by his body's unwillingness to allow him to do the things he would like to do with his life and for God. He has found his place in the world simply by volunteering several days per week at a Christian early learning center, spending hours on the floor and in the rocker with infants and toddlers. His own spirit, so frustrated and aggravated by his physical disability, is renewed each day with the gentleness of being God's agent around the smallest and most vulnerable among us.

5. Skip caffeine for a day or get a massage. Take the edge off. Marvel at the gentleness that emerges in your day as tension subsides. Watch as your pace slows and your attention allows you really to notice people around you. Interact with a new level of gentleness. Experience the healing grace of touch with a massage. Massage often helps release the tensions from unproductive grudges and hurts that prevent you from becoming the-best-version-of-yourself.

SELF-CONTROL

"... the fruit of the Spirit is love, joy, peace, patience, kindness, generosity, faithfulness, gentleness, SELF-CONTROL ..."
Galatians 5:22–23

Self-Control

9. YOUR BEST FRIEND

*This single verse of Scripture may well
be the crucial key to self-control.*

Question: What's the most important word to know if you want to become the-best-version-of-yourself?

Answer: *Self-control.*

Self-control determines whether you will have a life full of God. Without self-control, the-best-version-of-yourself will never be more than a dream.

There's a reason self-control arrives at the end of the list of the nine fruit God wants to produce in you: Self-control provides the key to enjoying all of the other eight fruit of God's Spirit. Self-control gives you the opportunity to *choose* to do those things that are healthy and helpful and to choose *not* to do those things that are harmful and destructive. Self-control gives you the possibility to be open to God's Spirit rather than resisting Him. Self-control gives you the strength to resist the temptations that lead you away from God and the-best-version-of-yourself. Self-control will be your best friend, and self-control comes from God.

God gives you the freedom to choose to work with or against His Spirit in your life. And self-control is the single greatest tool available to you to cooperate with God's dream for you. Countless times each day, you will have the opportunity to choose to exercise self-control or abandon it. That means that self-control, more than any of the other fruit of the Spirit, is the one fruit that you can partly control. Even better, through the wise use of self-control, you can use one fruit to cultivate the other eight fruit of the Spirit in your life. Self-control can lead to a greater abundance of the other fruit in you.

So, if self-control is so crucial and it comes from God, how do you excel at it? And how do you acquire it in the first place?

First, self-control can be a tough fruit to bear. You already know you are surrounded by a culture that discourages self-control. In fact, the world often encourages a total lack of it. Television shows feature contestants who revel in being completely out of control, politicians and celebrities swim in a sea of serial sexual relationships and jump from bed to bed almost by the week. Binge drinking has become normal behavior on college campuses, and birth control is distributed freely in middle schools.

In a world that mocks self-control and embraces a philosophy of "If it feels good, do it," how do you find an ounce of self-control? How do you learn to master your passions and temptations in order to live in God's Spirit and to become the-best-version-of-yourself? Good news! The Scriptures offer a marvelous prescription for how to abound in self-control.

Five Sacred Steps toward Self-control

1) Decide what you really want

It seems so simple and obvious. Ask yourself: "What do I really want in my life?"

If you could choose only one priority for your life, what would it be? A loving spouse? The blessings of children? Sobriety? Fabulous wealth? Success in your career?

Before you decide, remember the words of Jesus: *"Seek **first** the kingdom of God and his righteousness, and **all** these things will be given you besides."* (Matthew 6:33)

God makes it clear. *He* is the priority for your life. He comes first. If that is not the case, everything else will overwhelm you and compete for your affection. But with that decision made, all other blessings and fruit will begin to flow in your life. Without that decision, your life will shipwreck on the rocks of your own shifting wishes and ambitions.

Sue merely wanted happiness. In fact, she desired happiness more than anything else. In her mind, job stress, marital strain, the demands of her children, and the pressures of family all prevented her happiness. So Sue began to look for happiness in any place she could find. Eventually, she landed in an alcohol rehabilitation facility for her addiction to a substance she thought would help her escape those pressures and find the happiness she so desperately longed for. Her time in the rehabilitation center finally helped her to see that making a poor choice in what she really wanted in life had led to a loss of control. Sue had mistaken a good feeling, a quickened pulse, and high emotions for a meaningful and happy life. She failed to see that happiness comes from God. Choose Him first and happiness will follow. Seek happiness, however, and you will never find it.

The point is simple: If you deeply desire to become the-best-version-of-yourself, choose God above all else. If you want a life that produces fruit such as love, joy, and peace, make up your mind to desire God first, above all other things in your life.

2) Give your life over to Him

After choosing God as your first priority, give your life over to Him completely—every aspect, every part, every day, completely.

In doing so, discover the joy of being governed by God. Invite His Spirit to govern and control your life. Saint Paul captures how this works in one of the verses we began with in the introduction to this venture: *"I have been crucified with Christ; yet I live, no longer I, but Christ lives in me; insofar as I now live in the flesh, I live by faith in the Son of God who has loved me and given himself up for me."* (Galatians 2:20)

This single verse of Scripture may well be the crucial key to self-control. Make Jesus the Lord of life, and He will live in you. Following Christ means to be crucified with Him. Old passions and habits are put to death so that a new life can emerge. With Christ, you will live life in a new way, by faith in Him. Notice how the apostle Paul writes this verse regarding being crucified with Christ and living in a new way just a few chapters before he writes down the goal of the fruit of the Spirit. This verse on being crucified with Christ and living by faith in Him sets the stage for the-best-version-of-yourself by showing you how God works in your life.

First, Jesus gave Himself for you. He loved you first. Christ took the initiative.

Second, you accept that love and allow Him to be Lord of your life. That means putting past ways behind you and being crucified with Him. Your old way of doing things is put to death and replaced by His new way of love.

Third, Christ becomes the governor of your life and He directs your life through His Holy Spirit.

This is the goal of the Christian life, to have Jesus Christ through His Holy Spirit directing and governing every part of your life. Jesus is not merely one part of your life. Rather, He is life.

This is the basic step of faith. Faith means trust. When you trust God in Jesus Christ with this basic step of faith in place, you are set free from your own ways to discover the mighty power of God in your life.

Best of all, when the Holy Spirit begins to govern your life, self-control will naturally follow.

3) Seek His Spirit and His help in all that you do

Gaining self-control occurs daily, step by step. It is more like a slow cooker than a microwave. Learning to have self-control in what you say, how you act, what you watch, what you eat, and where you go emerges gradually. Day by day: *That* is how you give your life over to Him. And the more bits of your life that are given over to Him, the more Spirit-filled self-control is available to you.

How does this happen? Through the Holy Spirit. God promises to share His Holy Spirit with you. And the Holy Spirit is available to walk beside you each day, directing your steps and decisions, guiding your heart and your mind. He tells that to all of us over and over again.

Most of all, the Spirit invades our lives in the Eucharist. With the body and blood of Jesus, God is putting Himself in you, slowly transforming you into the-best-version-of-yourself. Receiving the Eucharist regularly and often will accelerate your relationship and dependence on the Holy Spirit.

The Holy Spirit also governs us when we pray.

Prayer is like marrow. Marrow is where your blood cells are produced, the blood cells that are life itself. In other words, marrow produces life at its most basic level. It also generates defenses against diseases and attackers of life. *Webster's* defines *marrow* as the "innermost, essential, choicest part." Your body cannot survive without marrow.

Prayer is your spiritual marrow. It is the marrow of your soul, the innermost, essential, choicest part of your life with God. Prayer generates life in your soul, and it provides defense against the things that attack the soul. Prayer is where you communicate with God, live in God, are formed by God, and pay attention to Him. Prayer plugs your soul into God Himself.

As your soul gets connected to God in prayer, you learn to shift from what you want to what God wants. Prayer is not so much about asking God as it is about becoming an entirely new and different person, the-best-version-of-yourself. Prayer changes us. And there lies the heart of self-control: learning to desire what God wants rather than what you want. Prayer makes God's mind available to you. That is why Saint Paul says, *"Pray without ceasing."* (1 Thess. 5:17)

The Holy Spirit guides you when you immerse yourself in the Scriptures.

Read the Word and be amazed at how your relationship with Him grows and matures, at how your conversion deepens. Self-control will result. Why? Because *"All Scripture is inspired by God and is useful for teaching, for refutation, for correction, and for training in righteousness, so that one who belongs to God may be competent, equipped for every good work."* (2 Tim. 3:16–17)

Scripture is inspired. Literally, it is in-spirited. It is spoken by God, breathed out by him. In other words, when you spend time in the Word, you spend time with God. He meets you there. And the results are staggering. Something happens to you and in you as you are taught and trained for righteousness and equipped for good works. You are conformed to God. The Scriptures are so saturated with His Spirit that we are changed by our study of them. We are changed to have the mind of Christ.

Very simply, Scripture helps you be crucified with Christ and to live a new life in Him alone. As that occurs, self-control results.

That's why God invites you to form a habit with the Bible. The Old Testament puts it this way:

Hear, O Israel: The Lord is our God; the Lord alone. You shall love the Lord your God with all your heart, and with all your soul, and with all your strength. Keep these words that I am commanding you today in your hearts. Recite them to your children and talk about them when you are home and when you are away, when you lie down and when you get up. Bind them as a sign on your hand, fix them as an emblem on your forehead, and write them on the doorposts of your house and on your gates. (Deut. 6:4–9 [NRSV])

Moses instructs the people of Israel to form a Bible habit. Write the words down. Talk about them with your children, at home and away and at all times of the day. In other words, saturate your life with the Bible, because then the Spirit will saturate you.

Finally, the Holy Spirit directs you through the support and encouragement of godly friends.

Twelve-step programs, such as Alcoholics Anonymous, have taught this same basic concept for years. If you want to find change in your life, change your playgrounds and playmates. Recovering alcoholics have no choice but to quit hanging around people and places that encourage them to drink or to give in to temptation. The application of this concept to your desire for self-control is obvious. If friends or places lead to your being out of control, then change your friends and places. The price is too high not to change. You are seeking to become the-best-version-of-yourself. Anything that stands in the way of that is beneath you.

The best way to cultivate self-control? Find the support and encouragement of other people who are also seeking to grow in God's Spirit to become the-best-version-of-themselves. Their encouragement and support will greatly strengthen your own desires and heart. You may find these people at your parish, perhaps in your neighborhood, even at your workplace. But you will know them when you meet them; they will have the same sense of purpose and direction that you do. And they will possess a desire both to help you and for you to help them.

Learn to rely on these people and gather their wisdom as God speaks through them to you as well. The Bible displays for us time and again the crucial role that our fellow followers can and should play in our own spiritual growth. Take a quick trip through the book of Acts. Notice how often the believers meet regularly with one another for prayer, worship, Bible study, and encouragement (e.g., Acts 2.42–47; 4.32–37; 13.1–3; 14.21–28). They help one another discern what the Spirit of God desires and where the Spirit is leading.

Being a Christian is a team sport. We are a part of a greater community, the body of Christ. This is what it means to be a part of the one, holy, catholic, and apostolic Church. We are bound together. And the Holy Spirit speaks to you through the lives and mouths of your fellow believers.

4) Replace old habits with new ones

As you learn to desire God first, to give your life completely over to Him, and to seek His Spirit in all that you do, you will develop new habits. Slowly, new habits will replace old ones. You may spend less time on the Internet and more time in prayer or in adoration. Perhaps you will watch less television and instead invest that time in people. You may redirect your weekends and orient them more around the Eucharist and around service than mere pleasure. Habits and things that used to control you in areas in which you lack self-control will soon be transformed by your newfound strength from God's governance. God's Spirit will take over and your new habits will become holier habits.

These new habits will allow God to change you and form you. Holy habits require effort; they take work. God's grace is not cheap. It is not always easy. But the Holy Spirit meets you there.

This is what the apostle Paul means when he says, *"Do you not know that in a race the runners all compete, but only one receives the prize? Run in such a way that you may win it. Athletes exercise self-control in all things; they do it to receive a perishable crown but we an imperishable one. So I do not run aimlessly, nor do I box as though beating the air; but I punish my body and enslave it."* (1 Cor. 9:24–27a [NRSV])

Successful athletes maintain a disciplined, self-controlled regimen of exercise and diet. They learn to put aside those habits that will prevent their success. They learn to develop habits that will advance their strength and prowess. The same is true for your spirit. To advance your spiritual strength, you will learn to develop holy habits that place you under the influence of God's Spirit. And when you do, you will be well on your way to becoming the-best-version-of-yourself, in training as if you were an Olympic athlete preparing for the competition. Nothing less than your best will do.

I will always remember the summer Olympics of 1996, and the gymnastics competition on July 23 of that year in downtown Atlanta, Georgia. Little Kerri Strug was taking her final turn at the vault in hopes of winning a gold medal, which she had not attained four years earlier in the Olympics. Even more, this was a gold medal the American women's gymnastics team had never won. Kerri Strug was the final hope. But she had suffered painful injuries that many observers thought would prevent her from even competing in this final turn.

You might remember the picture too, of Kerri vaulting over the horse with severe ligament and tendon damage in her ankle. She grimaced and struggled valiantly under great pain. And she nailed a flawless vault to propel the women to gold as a team for the first time ever. Kerri Strug instantly rocketed into remarkable fame, holding a special place in American memories. Magazines and television spots all showed that image of her standing there, courageous, brave, and victorious in spite of her pain.

Commentators remarked that she had become a national hero overnight. What few, if any, of those writers or announcers mentioned was how Kerri had been training for more than twelve years, seven hours per day, six days a week, taking only Sundays off. She trained with discipline, with vigor, and with passion—for twelve long years! To become an "overnight" sensation had taken twelve years of discipline and healthy habits.

Kerri Strug trained relentlessly for years just to be ready for that one moment.

Saint Paul reminds you in 1 Cor. 9:24–27 that you are seeking not some gold medal that will be forgotten over the years but rather an eternal crown, a crown of glory with the King of Glory, Jesus Christ Himself. Just as this world's athletes train to prepare for victory, you and I will work at growing closer to God, because that is the ultimate goal of our lives. We will train. We will develop holy habits like the Eucharist, prayer, Scripture, and godly friends in order to grow forward. We will train, and it will be worth it. First, we will become the-best-version-of-ourselves.

Second, we will gain entry into the Kingdom of God and become a part of His heavenly chorus, forever. And our holy habits now will pay off richly then.

5) Follow Him one day at a time

Finally, life shows that self-control will not emerge overnight. It takes time. It grows daily. God's Spirit takes over and begins to govern you. Change occurs in spurts, usually in small increments, occasionally in huge leaps—but always over time. To try to decide today to have God's governance or self-control every day for the rest of your life is a recipe for failure. Instead of trying to please God for the rest of your life, choose to make Him first just for today, this one day. That is a much simpler task, a more achievable goal: Seek him freshly today. Acknowledge Him each hour. Let the years ahead take care of themselves. Choose Him just for today. Self-control will soon follow, because it is digested much more easily in small, daily doses rather than in one lifetime bite.

Saint Peter phrased it this way: *"For this very reason, make every effort to supplement your faith with virtue, virtue with knowledge, knowledge with* **self-control, self-control** *with endurance, endurance with devotion, devotion with mutual affection, mutual affection with love . . ."* (2 Pt. 1:5–6)

Bit by bit, day by day, faith brings virtue, which brings knowledge, then self-control, godliness, and love. Each day, the change may be barely noticeable. Over time, however, the transformation is amazing and wonderful. You are becoming the-best-version-of-yourself.

Thomas Merton wrote, "How does an apple ripen? It just sits in the sun." In other words, a small, green apple cannot ripen in one night by tightening all its muscles and squinting its eyes and clenching its jaw in order to miraculously find itself the next morning turned into a wonderfully large, red apple, ripe and juicy. In the same way, our transformation in Christ Jesus does not occur overnight or in one big, momentous decision. Instead, it takes time. It takes effort. And it takes self-control.

When you do these things, when you take these five sacred steps, be sure to look around you. Love, joy, and peace will begin to pop up in your flower beds. Notice how patience, kindness, and goodness begin to blossom in your orchard. Faithfulness and gentleness will sprout up in your garden. All of these good fruit are fertilized by the same thing: self-control.

The key to self-control is to desire God. Your goal is to become the-best-version-of-yourself. And you know you cannot do it apart from God, for He made you to become just that. So, yearn for God's face and His presence. Desire to have a heart for pleasing Him and serving Him only. If you want to look like Jesus, the journey begins with self-control. The road to the-best-version-of-yourself begins with self-control.

GROWING A LIFE OF SELF-CONTROL

1. Add a regular prayer time to your life. Include a ten-minute conversation with God as the start to each of your days. Before anything else enters your mind in the morning, spend that time with God. Set the course for your day in His presence. Allow Him to chart that course and inspire you for the day's journey. Listen. Seek His Spirit and counsel. Ask for His strength for self-control. Grow in His Spirit and grace. Spend time with Him. There is no substitute.

2. Develop a Scripture habit in your life. Join a weekly or monthly Bible study at your parish. Buy a copy of *The One Year Bible* and use it to work your way through the Scriptures. Listen to the Bible on tape as a part of your daily commute. Participate in a Bible study in your neighborhood or with friends for several weeks. Find a way to have Scripture fill your life. Feast on the Word of God. Live in the Spirit.

3. Cultivate godly friends who will encourage your self-control. Become part of a men's group, a prayer team, a Bible study group, a mission team, a musical ensemble, or a neighborhood group who will offer wisdom, encouragement, and strength for you just as you do for them. Find friends who seek self-control and godliness. Live in the Spirit with them.

4. Give up a harmful habit and replace it with a healthier, or holier, one. If you use pornography, choose for one week to substitute time with the Scriptures for that unhealthy time. If you have friends who take you to places that lead you into wasteful behavior, sign up for a service team or a prayer group that meets at the exact same time. If you are addicted to cigarettes, find a partner who will encourage you in giving those up and spend time with you when the worst withdrawals and temptations come. If you overeat, find a way to spend time walking with friends at the time of day that you most often choose to overeat.

5. Grow in contentment with who you are, what you have, and who God is. Memorize Philippians 4:11–12 (NRSV) and recite it throughout the day when temptation to lose control threatens you. Draw strength from the well of faith deep within you. *"For I have learned to be content with whatever I have. I know what it is to have little, and I know what it is to have plenty. In any and all circumstances, I have learned the secret of being well-fed and of going hungry, of having plenty and of being in need."*

10. ABUNDANCE

"... the fruit of the Spirit is love, joy, peace, patience, kindness, generosity, faithfulness, gentleness, self-control..."

God has much in store for you. He has high hopes and big dreams for your life. God desires to bless you in every way with every spiritual blessing in heaven and on earth. He invites you to a new way of life. God wants to help you leave behind the corruption and disappointments of this world to become the-best-version-of-yourself. Best of all, the Holy Spirit stands waiting to help you.

Remember the self-evaluation that you began with in the Introduction? Turn back and look at your original score.

Now rate yourself again. How much do you see each of God's fruit prospering in your life today?

Love	1 • 2 • 3 • 4 • 5 • 6 • 7 • 8 • 9 • 10
Joy	1 • 2 • 3 • 4 • 5 • 6 • 7 • 8 • 9 • 10
Peace	1 • 2 • 3 • 4 • 5 • 6 • 7 • 8 • 9 • 10
Patience	1 • 2 • 3 • 4 • 5 • 6 • 7 • 8 • 9 • 10
Kindness	1 • 2 • 3 • 4 • 5 • 6 • 7 • 8 • 9 • 10
Generosity	1 • 2 • 3 • 4 • 5 • 6 • 7 • 8 • 9 • 10
Faithfulness	1 • 2 • 3 • 4 • 5 • 6 • 7 • 8 • 9 • 10
Gentleness	1 • 2 • 3 • 4 • 5 • 6 • 7 • 8 • 9 • 10
Self-control	1 • 2 • 3 • 4 • 5 • 6 • 7 • 8 • 9 • 10

Have you made progress in these nine weeks of study and reflection? Have you implemented one or more of the suggested real-life helps at the end of the chapters where you see the need for the most growth?

What an opportunity lies before you! In Christ, you have an invitation to a life full of love, joy and peace; a life bearing patience, kindness, and generosity; a life rich in faithfulness, gentleness, and self-control. And you will discover that the fruit of God's Spirit all complement one another so that the more one grows, the more the others will grow too. After all, each of the fruit comes from the same Spirit, God's Spirit. And best of all, the more your relationship with Christ matures and ripens, the more your life will bear a rich harvest of God's fruit.

I pray that you will seize the opportunity and take the steps to allow God's grace to make your life completely new. Even more, I pray that God will mold you into the-best-version-of-yourself, a follower of Jesus bearing fruit in every aspect of your life. The suggestions included in this book are designed to help you do just that.

Finally, allow the words of Saint Peter below to remind you: Jesus is inviting you to enter His eternal Kingdom. He has richly provided it for you. Enjoy the journey as you become exactly who God intends you to be: the-best-version-of-yourself.

His divine power has bestowed on us everything that makes for life and devotion, through the knowledge of him who called us by his own glory and power. Through these, he has bestowed on us the precious and very great promises, so that through them you may come to share in the divine nature, after escaping from the corruption that is in the world because of evil desire. . . . If these are yours and increase in abundance, they will keep you from being idle or unfruitful in the knowledge of our Lord Jesus Christ. . . .

For, in this way, **entry into the eternal kingdom of our Lord and savior Jesus Christ will be richly provided for you.**

(2 Peter 1:3–11)

NINE WORDS
Study Questions for Groups

Introduction

1. Memorize Galatians 5:22–23. Name the nine fruit of the Spirit.

2. How can we have these spiritual fruit in our lives?

3. How will the world know we belong to Jesus?

Love

1. What is another name for God's love?

2. How would you define agape love, in your own words?

3. How is agape love different from other types of love that we experience?

4. What is meant by the phrase "love is vertical"?

5. Why is it important that God loves us first?

6. What is meant by the phrase "love is horizontal"?

7. Read Luke 10:25–37. In what ways does the Samaritan exhibit agape love?

8. Read Mark 10:17–22. In what ways does Jesus exhibit agape love?

9. How is it possible to lavish agape love on someone and still have him or her go away sad?

10. How can Christians "love one another with recklessness"?

11. Explain the sentence "We have agape love in our lives only because God has shown His love for us in Jesus."

12. Name some practical examples of a love that will "cost us something."

Joy

1. The author writes, "While negativism is highly contagious, joy is not so contagious," and therefore, "joy must be cultivated." Why is this true in our world?

2. In Luke 2:10, the angel said, "I bring you good news of great joy for all people." How would you explain this "good news of great joy" to someone who does not understand?

3. How does Jesus bring joy to your life?

4. Part of the joy that Jesus brings to our lives is a freedom that is made possible by the empty tomb. How does Jesus's resurrection give us freedom?

5. The original Greek meaning of the word *rejoice* in 1 Peter 8:9 is "to leap for joy, exult, to show one's joy by leaping and skipping." What is it that we're supposed to be this joyful about? Do you feel this joyful? Why or why not?

6. From the parable of the talents in Matthew 25, how do we enter into the joy of our master?

7. What practical ways do you try to combat the truism "negative people breed negative people" in your own life? In the lives of your children?

Peace

1. Where do you need peace?

2. Finding peace with God is the first priority in our lives. How do we do this?

3. When we live in Jesus, we acquire peace, and that peace not only lives in us, it protects us. Can you give an example of this from your experience?

4. Why must we first have peace with God before we can have peace with ourselves?

5. In spiritual terms, who are you? What does this understanding have to do with peace in your life?

6. What is the difference between the spiritual fruit of peace in your life and the peace that one may get from Transcendental Meditation?

7. Read Romans 12:14–18. How does being at peace with God and at peace with ourselves allow us to live out these commands?

8. Read Matthew 5:9. We are called to be active, not passive, in our peace relationships with others. Give examples of how we can practice peace.

9. How does peace begin in our prayers?

Patience

1. There may be as many common sayings about patience as about any other desired quality. List several.

2. What biblical examples can you think of that demonstrate God's patience?

3. What about in your own life? How has God been patient with you?

4. The author describes three different kinds of patience. The

first is end-time patience. How would you describe this in your own words?

5. Because we Christians know the outcome of our future, how should we live differently than the world lives?

6. Read Hebrews 6:10–12. What role does trust play in developing kingdom patience in our lives?

7. Describe social patience.

8. Why does social patience blossom directly out of end-time patience?

9. "Bearing with one another," or social patience, is often linked with the ability to forgive. Explain this relationship.

10. How is the third type, personal endurance and patience, different from the other two types of patience?

11. How can God use suffering in our lives for our ultimate good?

12. God grows patience in every believer's life. In what part of your life is this truth most noticeable?

Kindness

1. Our natural disposition toward others is to view them as less important or valuable than we are. What trends have you noticed in our culture that show this to be true?

2. Without digging too deeply, give an example from your own life this past week of how this principle has proven true.

3. A few verses before Ephesians 2:7, Paul makes references to those who *"live in the passions of our flesh, carrying out the desires of the body and the mind, and were by nature children of wrath."* How is it possible to view those in our society who may fit that

description as equal to or more important than you? Why is it critical to be able to see the "unlovable" in that light?

4. What do you think God's usual frame of mind is toward you? Toward the world?

5. Read Romans 2:1–4 again. If we truly show no condemnation of those around us, manifesting the fruit of God's kindness, how might that encourage someone to repent?

6. Evangelization has been described as "one beggar showing another beggar where to find bread." Why might a hungry beggar be more receptive to the Gospel when it's handed to him by another beggar as opposed to by a different source?

7. Who are the people around you who look up to you? How can you be another "beggar" to them?

8. Describe the kindness of Jesus with His disciples.

9. Why does it take "courage to be kind," as the author states?

10. Review 1 Peter 2:1–3. What may turn a good action into a righteous action?

11. One can easily be more envious of those who have more "stuff." How does God see those folks, and how might looking at them through His lens help your own attitude?

Generosity

1. What happens when we "miss the mark"?

2. What are the three ways Jesus uses mercy to teach about God's goodness?

3. When we sin, rather than sentence us to death, what does God do? Why?

4. What lies at the heart of being a Christian? Why does that make sense?

5. How is the world viewed through God's eyes? Why is it so hard for us to do likewise?

6. If "giving is joy," as the author states, why is it so difficult for us to give joyfully?

7. Compare life lived in the flesh to life lived in the Spirit. Which would you prefer? Why?

Faithfulness

1. What is the first image that comes to mind when you say the word faithful? Why?

2. What does it mean to be a faithful employee?

3. What are the attributes of a faithful God?

4. Romans 4:21 says that Abraham was *"fully convinced that God was able to do what He had promised."* List several biblical promises God has made to us as believers.

5. Faithfulness means trusting God, which is the foundation of our Christian faith journey. How can we grow in our ability to trust the Lord?

6. Read Matthew 25:14–30 again. The master, representing God, confronts the third servant, who views the master as a "hard man" and is terrified of him, wanting only to run from him. What might lead someone to feel that way about God?

7. How might you minister to a person like that?

8. The master entrusted great wealth to all three servants. What are the four examples the author gives of ways God gifts us?

9. Name two ways you could better manage the time God has entrusted to you.

10. We all have some talent or special ability with which God has gifted us. Think of yours, and how you could better use that talent to glorify Him.

11. List the two examples the author cites of ways we can glorify God and produce a return on His investment in us.

12. Again, referring to the parable of the talents, the author states, "God encourages His people to take risks to share the Gospel." Give an example of when the Holy Spirit has nudged you in this regard. Why do we sometimes resist those prompts?

13. There is an element of perseverance in faithfulness. How did Fr. Caj demonstrate this? How is such perseverance possible?

14. Fr. Caj has a deep loyalty to Christ. Would you describe yourself as loyal to the Savior?

Gentleness

1. What images in our culture come to mind with the words *gentleness* and *meekness?*

2. Some people describe gentleness as a wild horse that has been tamed or brought under control. How might this example apply to your faith journey?

3. Biblical gentleness comes only from God. Read Acts 22:3–10 and describe in your own words the almost instantaneous change in Paul's character toward gentleness.

4. Sometimes we can understand a concept better by seeing an example of the opposite. Read John 18:8–11. How is Peter not displaying biblical gentleness in this passage?

5. How does Jesus epitomize biblical gentleness in John 19:7–11?

6. How is biblical meekness a sign of strength?

7. What is the relationship between gentleness and humility?

8. Do you agree that "the world is full of arrogant, pushy, self-righteous Christians"? Why are all of us at times "eager to point out the sins and failures" of the people around us?

9. Why is a gentle spirit essential in sharing your faith with non-believers?

10. Do you know of any 310-year-old grudges? How can God's growing spirit of gentleness in a believer begin the restoration process?

11. Using the example of Joseph, the author writes that God shaped his spirit with such gentleness that Joseph is able to tell his brothers, "So it was not you who sent me into Egypt but God." How can your gentle spirit help other Christians to grow deeper in their own faith?

12. True or false: "Godly gentleness means never getting angry." Explain your answer.

13. At least three of the author's tips suggest a mind-body connection when it comes to a spirit of gentleness. Have you seen this in your own life?

Self-control

1. Self-control is listed as the last of the fruit of the spirit. Why would it be a good candidate for first?

2. Why is it the hardest fruit to enjoy?

3. List the five biblical steps toward self-control. Apply them to your life.

4. What are the priorities in your life?

5. What is "spiritual marrow"? Why is it so important?

6. What is the key to self-control?